Contents

Greatest Ever?

Greatest. That's a word heard all the time in sports. For some people, "The Greatest" will always be the late boxing legend **Muhammad Ali**. (That was one of his nicknames.) For others, the GOAT (Greatest of All Time) was a label put on NBA superstar **Michael Jordan**. But as 2016 wrapped up and 2017 rolled on, many experts were using that word to describe the whole sports world. In fact, you could easily make a case that this was the **GREATEST YEAR IN SPORTS** . . . ever.

Start with the Chicago Cubs. They had not won a World Series in 108 years! But in 2016, they thrilled their loyal fans by beating the Cleveland Indians in one of the greatest Game 7s of all time.

A couple of months later, Clemson rolled to a surprising national title with one of the greatest finishes in college football history. **DeShaun Watson** threw the winning TD pass to defeat mighty Alabama with just one second left in the game.

In early February, **Tom Brady** (a GOAT himself) led the New England Patriots to the greatest comeback in Super Bowl history. Brady rallied his team from 25 points down in the final quarter and won in overtime.

Down Under, tennis ace **Serena Williams** captured the Australian Open to set a new record for Grand Slam titles.

In women's college hoops, the University of Connecticut won 111 games in a row—the greatest streak ever. (Unfortunately, they lost what would have been No. 112 in the NCAA semifinals!)

Tom Brady was a Super Bowl hero.

Serena Williams won her record 23rd Open era Grand Slam at the 2017 Australian Open.

In the NBA, the Golden State Warriors, led by **Stephen Curry** and **Kevin Durant**, played so well while winning their second title in three years that some experts put them among the greatest teams ever.

Does winning two Champions League titles in a row make Real Madrid one of the greatest soccer teams ever? Some could argue that point, but almost everyone agrees that star striker **Cristiano Ronaldo** is among the all-time best.

Was the WNBA's final game the greatest ever played in the 20-year history of the league? The LA Sparks beat the Minnesota Lynx by one point in what some called an "instant classic."

Usain Bolt is clearly the greatest sprinter of all time, but he couldn't finish his last race. Sometimes, even the greatest can't be great all the time!

What was your greatest memory of this year in sports? We hope we included it in here. After you read all the way through, head out to the field or the gym or the park and create your own greatest moment in sports!

TOP 10

MOMENTS IN SPORTS
SEPTEMBER 2016 ▶ AUGUST 2017

Some experts have called this 12 months of sports the greatest ever. You be the judge! This Top 10 section highlights the best of the best. Find more details on all of them inside the book, too.

This year really did seem to have a huge number of incredible moments. It kicked off with baseball's biggest all-time losers becoming the sport's all-time champions, breaking a 108-year losing streak. Then the NFL featured the biggest Super Bowl comeback and first Super Bowl overtime ever, with a new player crowned Greatest of All Time. The NBA featured a team some called the greatest of all time, too, but it was a one-man wrecking machine that drew the most attention.

NASCAR crowned another all-time, record-tying great. Connecticut's women's hoops team set its own, probably unbeatable, record. And in soccer, an international hero helped set an international first.

First . . . all-time . . . greatest . . . record-breaking: Sports fans heard those words all year long. But that's what we love about sports. As soon as every new season begins, the chance of something even greater happening is just around the corner!

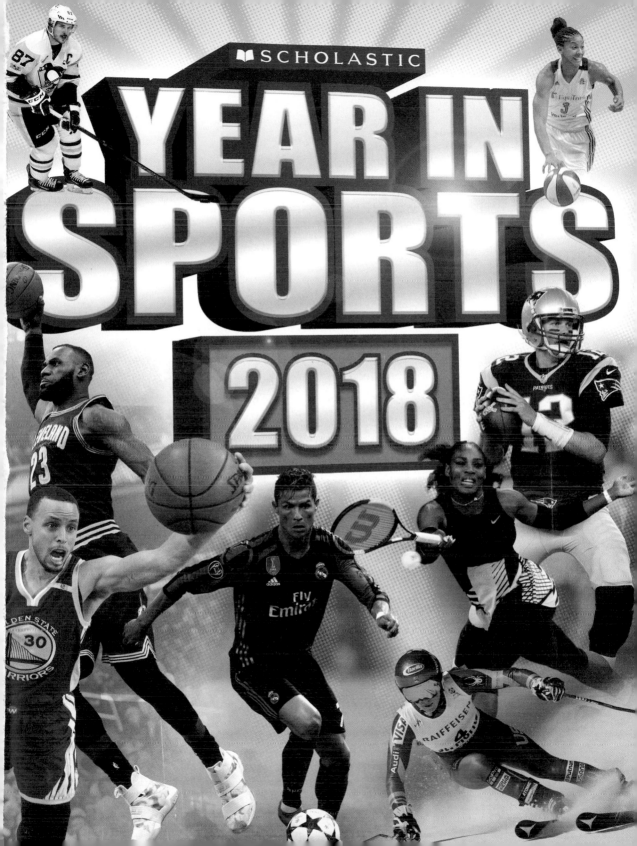

ISBN 978-1-338-18425-9

10 9 8 7 6 5 4 3 2 1   17 18 19 20 21

Printed in the U.S.A.   40
First edition, December 2017

Produced by Shoreline Publishing Group LLC

Due to the publication date, records, results, and statistics are current as of August 2017.

UNAUTHORIZED: This book is not sponsored by or affiliated with the athletes, teams, or anyone involved with them.

10 SUPER STREAK *They were unstoppable. The University of Connecticut women's basketball team* won 111 games in a row from 2014 to 2017. No other men's or women's team in any major sport has matched that amazing number. (And UConn has the second-longest streak for women's hoops, too, at 90 games.) But while the streak was impressive, it wasn't enough. The Huskies were upset by Mississippi State in the NCAA semifinals. Time to start a new streak!

9 PATRIOT POWER *Sports fans love a debate. They love to argue who is the all-time greatest. In 2017, Patriots quarterback* **Tom Brady** *probably ended that argument in the NFL. He led New England to the biggest comeback in NFL playoff history, won his record fourth Super Bowl MVP award, and became the first QB to win five Super Bowls. Debate over!*

8 **RONALDO'S REAL** *In UEFA Champions League soccer, no team had won back-to-back titles since the European club tournament changed to its present format in 1995. Real Madrid broke that streak, winning in 2017 after triumphing in 2016. Real Madrid was led by Cristiano Ronaldo, who scored twice in the final-game win over Juventus of Italy.*

STUNNING SERENA *Women's tennis has seen some amazing athletes over the years. But none can top **Serena Williams**. She cemented her spot atop the all-time list by winning the 2017 Australian Open. That gave her 23 career Grand Slam singles titles—a new record since tennis moved to the Open era in 1968. Serena's year got even better several months later, when she announced that she and her fiancé, Alexis Ohanian, were expecting a child!*

6 **WONDERFUL WESTBROOK** *The triple-double is a unique basketball stat. This rare feat happens when a player reaches double digits in three stat categories in one game. In 2017, Oklahoma City's Russell Westbrook went triple-double crazy! The multitalented guard set a new NBA record with 42 triple-doubles. To top it off, he averaged a triple-double for the whole season: 31.6 points, 10.7 rebounds, and 10.4 assists per game. Only the great Oscar Robertson did that—way back in 1961–62.*

5 **MAJOR MASTER** *In golf, there always seems to be a player with great skills and lots of big wins but no major championships. Before the 2017 Masters, that was* **Sergio García.** *The Spanish star had won nine times on the PGA Tour and 30 times around the world, and he helped win the Ryder Cup five times for Europe. But he had never won a major. That streak ended in Augusta when he beat Justin Rose in a playoff to win the famous green jacket.*

4

SUPER SEVEN

In NASCAR, there are two legendary names atop the all-time list: Richard Petty and Dale Earnhardt Sr., who each won seven season championships. Change that to there were two names. After his 2016 triumph, Jimmie Johnson added his name to the list of seven-time NASCAR champs.

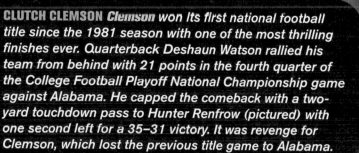

3

CLUTCH CLEMSON *Clemson* won its first national football title since the 1981 season with one of the most thrilling finishes ever. Quarterback Deshaun Watson rallied his team from behind with 21 points in the fourth quarter of the College Football Playoff National Championship game against Alabama. He capped the comeback with a two-yard touchdown pass to Hunter Renfrow (pictured) with one second left for a 35–31 victory. It was revenge for Clemson, which lost the previous title game to Alabama.

DURANT'S DECISION

2

Kevin Durant made the right choice when he signed with the Golden State Warriors for the 2016–17 season. Already an all-time star, Durant was missing one thing: a championship ring. He bought into the Warriors' team-first game plan, battled a midseason injury, and finally stood atop the NBA. He was the best player in an NBA Finals packed with great players. Golden State won its second title in three years, defeating the LeBron James-led Cleveland Cavaliers in five games.

1

CUBS CLASSIC *For more than a century, the Chicago Cubs were baseball's—and the sports world's—lovable losers. They went year after year without a shot at the top. Even when they got close, they always found a way to lose. All that ended in 2016. A collection of young talent, helped by some key veterans, finally came together to win the team's first World Series since 1908. They won one of the most exciting Game 7s ever, beating the Cleveland Indians in 10 innings to set off a Chicago-wide celebration.*

PATRIOTS POWER!
New England Patriots RB James White burrowed through three Atlanta Falcons defenders to score the winning TD in Super Bowl LI. New England made a historic comeback, forcing the first Super Bowl overtime. Pats QB Tom Brady took his place as an all-time great with his fourth Super Bowl MVP trophy. The game capped a remarkable season. Turn the page to read all about it!

Super Season!

The 2016 NFL season started with New England quarterback **Tom Brady** on the sidelines after being suspended. It ended with him holding the Super Bowl trophy . . . again. Along the way, the NFL provided a ton of amazing stories for fans and players alike.

Brady's suspension was certainly the biggest story at the beginning of the season. He sat for four games as a result of what happened during the 2015 AFC Championship Game. The NFL said that Brady had been involved in deflating footballs before that game. But the Patriots still won three of the four games he missed. When he returned, Brady was still the best. In his 12 regular-season games, he threw 28 TD passes and a career-low 2 interceptions.

In the AFC West, a pair of teams seemed destined for playoff success. The Kansas City Chiefs rolled to 12 wins, helped by a stingy defense. The Oakland Raiders returned to their glory days and won the division. But they suffered a huge blow when QB **Derek Carr** went down with a leg injury. Without him, they lost in the first round of the playoffs.

Raiders QB Derek Carr

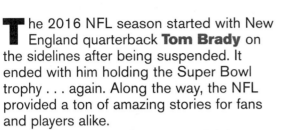

The Pittsburgh Steelers had a solid season, led by the "Killer Bs"—QB **Ben Roethlisberger**, RB **Le'Veon Bell**, and WR **Antonio Brown**, who led the AFC with 106 catches.

Also in the AFC, the Cleveland Browns beat the San Diego Chargers! Why is that news? Because it was the only game Cleveland won all season.

In the NFC, the big story was the amazing rookie duo from the Dallas Cowboys. QB **Dak Prescott** took over for injured star **Tony Romo** and pretty much put Romo out of a job. Prescott started his career by throwing a record 176 straight passes without an interception, leading the Cowboys to 13 wins. He got a lot of help from a fellow rookie, RB **Ezekiel Elliott**, who led the NFL with 1,631 rushing yards.

The other surprise team in the NFC was the New York Giants. They snuck up on everyone, using a strong defense that gave up a conference-low 284 points, and won 11 games.

On the other side of the ball, the Atlanta Falcons scored 540 points in 2016, the seventh most in league history. **Matt Ryan** earned NFL MVP honors by getting the ball as often as he could to **Julio Jones** and a crew of talented receivers.

Once again, the Green Bay Packers and Seattle Seahawks had outstanding seasons. This time, though, their star QBs—**Aaron Rodgers** and **Russell Wilson**—couldn't carry them to the big prize.

In the end, the Falcons' powerful offense and the Patriots' overall excellence led to a Super Bowl matchup that will be talked about for years. Relive all the excitement on page 27.

ON THE MOVE!

In 2016, the Rams played their first season back in Los Angeles after moving from St. Louis. In 2017, LA got a second team. The San Diego Chargers moved north, returning to the city where they started in 1960. The Oakland Raiders also got approval to move to Las Vegas, probably in 2019. Time to buy new gear, fans!

2016 Final Regular-Season Standings

AFC EAST		NFC EAST	
New England Patriots	14–2	Dallas Cowboys	13–3
Miami Dolphins	10–6	New York Giants	11–5
Buffalo Bills	7–9	Washington Redskins	8–7–1
New York Jets	5–11	Philadelphia Eagles	7–9
AFC NORTH		**NFC NORTH**	
Pittsburgh Steelers	11–5	Green Bay Packers	10–6
Baltimore Ravens	8–8	Detroit Lions	9–7
Cincinnati Bengals	6–9–1	Minnesota Vikings	8–8
Cleveland Browns	1–15	Chicago Bears	3–13
AFC SOUTH		**NFC SOUTH**	
Houston Texans	9–7	Atlanta Falcons	11–5
Tennessee Titans	9–7	Tampa Bay Buccaneers	9–7
Indianapolis Colts	8–8	New Orleans Saints	7–9
Jacksonville Jaguars	3–13	Carolina Panthers	6–10
AFC WEST		**NFC WEST**	
Kansas City Chiefs	12–4	Seattle Seahawks	10–5–1
Oakland Raiders	12–4	Arizona Cardinals	7–8–1
Denver Broncos	9–7	St. Louis Rams	4–12
San Diego Chargers	5–11	San Francisco 49ers	2–14

2016 Playoffs

Wild-Card Playoffs

Texans 27, Raiders 14

Without injured QB **Derek Carr**, Oakland could not get their offense going. Houston's **Johnathan Joseph** had 10 tackles and **Jadeveon Clowney** picked off a pass to help the Texans win the game.

Rawls's rambles led the way for Seattle.

Seahawks 26, Lions 6

Thomas Rawls set a Seattle playoff record with 161 yards rushing. His teammate **Paul Richardson** made a one-handed TD grab, and Seattle rolled over the Lions. Detroit continued a sad streak—it has not won a road playoff game since 1957!

Steelers 30, Dolphins 12

The Killer Bs struck the Dolphins! QB **Ben Roethlisberger** threw a pair of TD passes to **Antonio Brown**, while RB **Le'Veon Bell** scored twice as well. Bell also set a team postseason record with 167 yards rushing.

Packers 38, Giants 13

Green Bay QB **Aaron Rodgers** continued his super-hot play, throwing 4 TD passes and running the team's winning streak to seven games. The most memorable was a 42-yard Hail Mary pass on the final play of the first half. **Randall Cobb** caught it in the end zone behind a crowd of defenders.

Divisional Playoffs

Falcons 36, Seahawks 20

In this battle of the "birds," the Falcons flew highest. Atlanta's offense averaged 33.8 points per game during the season, and it

Very special teams: Mason Crosby blasted this 51-yard field goal to win for Green Bay.

kept it up in this game. QB **Matt Ryan** threw 3 TD passes to lead the way to victory.

Patriots 34, Texans 16

Houston kept it close—trailing by only four after two quarters—but New England shut them down in the second half. It was not the Patriots' prettiest win, but they did what they needed to do against the league's No. 1 defense.

Steelers 18, Chiefs 16

Chris Boswell of the Steelers set an NFL postseason record by hitting 6 field goals in one game. The Chiefs nearly tied it on a two-point conversion, but it was called back for a holding penalty. The cold and wind—and tough D—kept the score low.

Packers 34, Cowboys 31

This classic contest included three field goals of more than 50 yards each in the last 93 seconds! What an ending! Green Bay knocked off Dallas when **Mason Crosby** nailed a 51-yard field goal to win it on the game's final play. He had a 56-yard kick on the previous drive, but the Cowboys' **Dan Bailey** then tied the game with a 52-yarder! The Packers' win hid a great comeback by Dallas and QB **Dak Prescott**, after the Cowboys had been down by 18 points down in the first half.

Championship Games

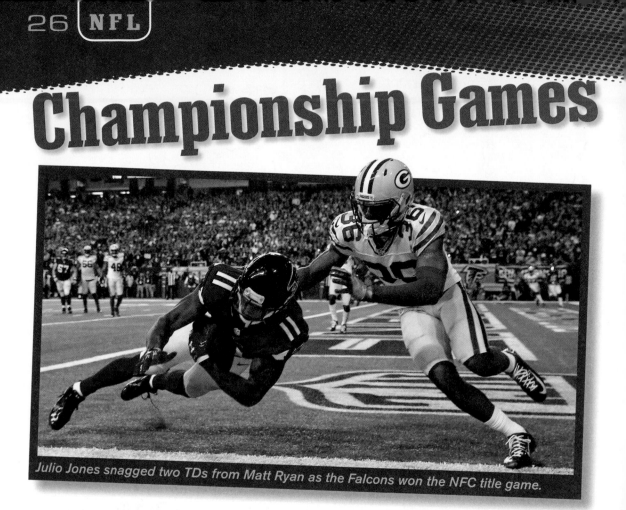

Julio Jones snagged two TDs from Matt Ryan as the Falcons won the NFC title game.

NFC

Falcons 44, Packers 21

How much did **Matt Ryan** want to win this game? So much that he actually ran for a touchdown, his first since 2012. He added 4 TD passes and 392 passing yards to lead Atlanta to a win over Green Bay. WR **Julio Jones** had an awesome game, catching 9 passes for 180 yards, capped by a 73-yard catch-and-run TD that made the score 31–0. Ryan and his teammates headed to the Super Bowl for only the second time in Falcons history.

AFC

Patriots 36, Steelers 17

The **Tom Brady** Victory Tour continued with a convincing win over Pittsburgh. Brady set a postseason career high with 384 passing yards, along with 3 TD passes. The surprise star was WR **Chris Hogan**. He set a New England playoff record with 180 receiving yards while also catching a pair of TDs. Pittsburgh did lose star RB **Le'Veon Bell** early in the game due to injury, but it probably wouldn't have changed the outcome. Brady & Co. headed to Super Bowl LI to continue the tour!

Super Bowl LI

Brady was the first QB with 5 SB wins.

When you have the greatest QB in NFL history on your side, you usually don't worry. But even the most devoted Patriots fans were probably a little nervous during Super Bowl LI. By midway through the third quarter, Atlanta led New England 28–3. Falcons QB **Matt Ryan** was having a super day. Also, for the first time all season, New England had given up a pick-six—Atlanta's **Robert Alford** did the honors.

And then there was this fact: In 93 previous NFL postseason games in which a team led by at least 19 points entering the fourth quarter, that team went on to win the game. The Patriots trailed by as many as *25 points*, and they were losing 28–9 entering the fourth quarter.

No problem.

SUPER BOWL LI

TEAM	1Q	2Q	3Q	4Q	OT	FINAL
FALCONS	0	21	7	0	0	28
PATRIOTS	0	3	6	19	6	34

SCORING

2Q: ATL Freeman 5 run (Bryant kick)

2Q: ATL Hooper 19 pass from Ryan (Bryant kick)

2Q: ATL Alford 82 int return (Bryant kick)

2Q: NE Gostkowski 41 FG

3Q: ATL Coleman 6 pass from Ryan (Bryant kick)

3Q: NE White 5 pass from Brady (kick failed)

4Q: NE Gostkowski 33 FG

4Q: NE Amendola 6 pass from Brady (White run)

4Q: NE White 1 run (Brady-Amendola pass)

OT: NE White 2 run

New England put together perhaps the greatest comeback in the history of championship games. **Tom Brady** led the Pats to 25 unanswered points. That included TD passes to **James White** and **Danny Amendola**, plus a pair of successful two-point conversions. The last of those tied the score at 28 and led to the first overtime in Super Bowl history.

In OT, the Patriots got the ball first—and last. Brady drove the Patriots down the field to the 2-yard line. Then White punched the ball in, barely crossing the goal line to hand the Patriots the unlikely title 34–28.

Patriots fans booed NFL Commissioner **Roger Goodell** until he handed the Lombardi Trophy to New England owner **Robert Kraft**. Then they awarded Kraft and game MVP Brady the opposite: a huge roar of approval.

2016 Stats Leaders

1,631 RUSHING YARDS
Ezekiel Elliott, Cowboys

18 RUSHING TDS
LeGarrette Blount, Patriots

5,208 PASSING YARDS
Drew Brees, Saints

40 PASSING TDS
Aaron Rodgers, Packers

107 RECEPTIONS
◄◄◄**Larry Fitzgerald**, Cardinals

1,448 RECEIVING YARDS
T.Y. Hilton, Colts

14 RECEIVING TDS
Jordy Nelson, Packers

38 FIELD GOALS
Justin Tucker, Ravens

158 POINTS
Matt Bryant, Falcons

15.5 SACKS
Vic Beasley, Falcons

7 INTERCEPTIONS
Casey Hayward, Chargers

167 TACKLES
Bobby Wagner, Seahawks

Award Winners

NFL MVP
MATT RYAN QB ▶▶▶
FALCONS

DEFENSIVE PLAYER OF THE YEAR
KHALIL MACK LB
RAIDERS

OFFENSIVE ROOKIE OF THE YEAR
DAK PRESCOTT QB
COWBOYS

DEFENSIVE ROOKIE OF THE YEAR
JOEY BOSA DE
CHARGERS

COMEBACK PLAYER OF THE YEAR
JORDY NELSON WR
PACKERS

COACH OF THE YEAR
JASON GARRETT
COWBOYS

WALTER PAYTON NFL MAN OF THE YEAR (COMMUNITY SERVICE)
LARRY FITZGERALD WR
CARDINALS
ELI MANNING QB
GIANTS

13

Okay, that's not really a BIG number, but it *was* a record. **Matt Ryan** threw at least one TD pass to 13 different Atlanta Falcons in 2016—the most by one QB in a single season. And that's a good lesson in sharing!

1st Quarter

WEEKS 1-4

Wentz (right) helped knock off Big Ben.

★ Comeback City: Kansas City set a team record by coming back from a 21-point deficit to defeat the San Diego Chargers in overtime 33–27.

★ New Homes: The Rams returned to Los Angeles after moving to St. Louis in 1994. A sellout crowd of 91,000 fans packed the Coliseum. Their support helped the Rams upset the Seahawks 9–3. Also, the Vikings played their first game in a new stadium and pulled off an upset. New QB **Sam Bradford** threw two touchdown passes in Minnesota's 17–14 win over Green Bay.

★ Who Needs Brady?: The Patriots won their second straight without suspended star **Tom Brady**. **Jimmy Garoppolo** threw three touchdowns. But he had to leave with a shoulder injury, so third-stringer **Jacoby Brissett** took over to guide them to another score. The Pats beat Miami, 31–24.

★ Super Déjà Vu: As he had in Super Bowl 50, Denver linebacker **Von Miller** pulled off a strip sack for a key score. This time it was against Colts QB **Andrew Luck** and clinched Denver's 34–20 win.

★ Busy Guy!: **Terrelle Pryor** deserved a rest after a very busy day. The Browns' coaches put him in for 14 plays in a shotgun formation. He ran, passed, and caught 8 passes. He also played a down at safety to help prevent a long pass late in the first half. He was the first player since 1964 with at least three catches, passes, and runs in the same game. Yet, Pryor's Browns lost to the Dolphins, 30–24, in overtime.

★ Rookie Surprise: The Eagles shocked the Steelers thanks to a great game by their defense and super play from rookie QB **Carson Wentz**. The No. 2 overall pick in 2016 threw for 301 yards and 2 TDs in a convincing 34–3 win.

★ Indy Comeback: The Colts' **Andrew Luck** connected with **T.Y. Hilton** on a 63-yard game-winner that clinched Indy's 26–22 win. San Diego had taken the lead only moments before Luck's big strike.

★ Flying Falcon: Atlanta beat Carolina 48–33, and, for the first time in NFL history, a team had a 300-yard receiver (**Julio Jones**) and a 500-yard passer (**Matt Ryan**) in the same game.

2nd Quarter
WEEKS 5-8

★ V for Victory: And for Vikings! Minnesota became the last undefeated team in the league with another dominating defensive effort. They beat Houston 31–13, helped by a punt-return TD from **Marcus Sherels**.

★ Welcome Back!: Brady didn't have any rust on him after his four-week suspension ended. He threw for 406 yards and 3 touchdowns as the Patriots beat the Browns 33–13.

★ Rookies in Charge: Dallas won its fourth game under the leadership of rookie QB **Dak Prescott**, beating Cincinnati 28–14. **Ezekiel Elliott** became the first Cowboys rookie with three straight 100-yard games.

★ Comeback King: Trailing in the fourth quarter? No problem for Seattle QB **Russell Wilson**. For the 20th time in his career, he led the Seahawks to a come-from-behind victory. This time, he set up **Steven Hauschka**'s 44-yard field goal, the winning points in their 26–24 win over Atlanta.

★ 400 Again: **Drew Brees** had 465 passing yards in the Saints' win over the Panthers. It was Brees's 15th career game above 400 yards. The effort a helped the Saints win 41–38. It was not all Brees, however, though he did also have 4 TD passes by Brees. The Saints got a 52-yard, final-minute field goal by **Wil Lutz** to seal the victory.

★ Then There Were None: Minnesota lost its first game of the season as Philadelphia's defense shut down the Vikings. A second-quarter kickoff TD return got the Eagles started. The D did the rest, spoiling the return of former Eagle Sam Bradford. The Eagles won 21–10.

★ Great Company: Miami RB **Jay Ajayi** became only the fourth NFL runner ever with back-to-back 200-yard games. His 214 yards helped Miami overcome an 11-point deficit and defeat Buffalo 28–25.

★ Rule Breakers Win!: The Raiders set a new NFL record by committing 23 penalties and still managing to beat the Buccaneers 30–24 in overtime. Oakland QB **Derek Carr** set a team record with 513 passing yards—though of course he had nearly a whole extra quarter to do it!

Ajayi pounded out two 200-yarders!

3rd Quarter
WEEKS 9-12

✱ Going Long!: A list of big-yardage plays turned the tide in many games in Week 9:

➤ **Joe Flacco** connected with Ravens teammate **Mike Wallace** on a team-record 95-yard TD to lead Baltimore to a 21–14 win over Pittsburgh.

➤ **Kenyan Drake**'s 96-yard kickoff return helped Miami beat the Jets.

➤ **Jordan Todman** got the Colts off to a great start. His 99-yard kickoff return came on the game's first play. Indianapolis held on for a 31–26 win over Green Bay.

✱ A New Way to Score: In 2015, the NFL added a rule that gives two points to a defensive team that blocks an extra-point attempt and returns it all the way. In Week 10, Denver's **Will Parks** became the first to win a game that way, picking up a

High-scoring Beckham kept up his pace.

blocked kick and running it back 84 yards. Those were the final points in a thrilling 25–23 Denver win over New Orleans.

✱ Classic Battle: In one of the best games of the season so far, the Cowboys and Steelers went through seven lead changes. Dallas rookie RB **Ezekiel Elliott** ran for two scores in the game's final two minutes. The last TD, for 32 yards, came after **Ben Roethlisberger** of the Steelers had thrown a perfect TD strike to **Antonio Brown** after faking that he was going to spike the ball. The 35–30 win was Dallas's eighth straight, matching the team record.

✱ Good Times in New Orleans: The Saints threw a scoring party in New Orleans and invited the Rams to watch. **Drew Brees** threw for 4 scores and dove in himself for a fifth as the Saints romped 49–21.

✱ Big Leg!: **Justin Tucker** of Baltimore became the first kicker to boot 3 field goals of 50-plus yards in the first half of a game. He helped the Ravens to a 19–14 win over the Bengals.

✱ Two for Beckham: Giants receiver **Odell Beckham Jr.** continued his hot play. He caught two TD passes in New York's 27–13 victory over winless Cleveland. That gave "ODB" five scores in four games.

✱ Historic Game: In Kansas City's 30–27 overtime win over Denver, KC's **Tyreek Hill** scored on a kickoff return, a run, and a reception. It was the first time since 1965 that an NFL player had done so in one game.

4th Quarter
WEEKS 13-17

✱ Rampaging Raiders: Oakland continued its hot season with a comeback win over Buffalo. The Raiders trailed 24–9 in the third quarter before scoring 29 straight points to win 38–24.

✱ Miami Mashers: Baltimore's Joe Flacco set a team record with 36 completions, including four for TDs, which helped the Ravens defeat Miami 38–6.

✱ Snow Problem!: Pittsburgh's **Le'Veon Bell** had no trouble dashing through the snow in Buffalo. He set a team record with 236 rushing yards while scoring 3 touchdowns. The Steelers beat the Bills, 27–20.

✱ Another Detroit Squeaker: For the eighth time this season—a new NFL record—the Lions came from behind to win in the fourth quarter. This time, it was QB **Matt Stafford** doing the honors. He rumbled in for a seven-yard TD run, and the Lions overcame the Bears 20–17.

✱ Dallas Goes Down: The Cowboys' 11-game winning streak ended the same way it started—with a loss to the Giants. New York's defense bottled up the Dallas attack. Odell Beckham Jr. caught a 61-yard TD pass, and the Giants held on to win 10–7. It was the Cowboys' second loss of the season, and both were to the Giants.

✱ Record-Setter: New England's 16–3 win over Denver gave it eight straight AFC

Stafford dove into the end zone to beat the Bears.

East titles. That's a new NFL record streak for divisional championships.

✱ Raider Nation!: The Raiders avoided setting their own NFL record. They had gone 14 seasons without a playoff spot— the second-longest streak ever. Their 19–16 win over San Diego clinched their first playoff spot since 2002.

✱ W for Cleveland: Joy in Ohio! Cleveland won its first game of the season! The Browns avoided going 0–16 when San Diego missed a game-tying field goal. The Browns hung on to win 20–17.

✱ Good Call!: When Green Bay was 4–6, QB **Aaron Rodgers** said, "We just have to run the table to win the division." That would mean winning all six remaining games. On the final Sunday of the season, Rodgers made it come true. Green Bay beat Detroit 31–24 and won the NFC North.

NFL Milestones

Here's a sampling of some of the interesting new records set in the 2016 season.

Late Magic: Detroit set an NFL record by winning eight games in which they were trailing in the fourth quarter or OT.

Record Streak: New England's AFC East title was its eighth straight—the longest streak in NFL history.

Sore Arm?: Philadelphia QB **Carson Wentz** set a rookie record with 379 completions.

Record Receiver: Pittsburgh WR **Antonio Brown** had 481 catches from 2013–2016, the most ever in a four-year span.

Mr. Dependable: Indianapolis RB **Frank Gore** recorded his 11th straight season with more than 1,200 yards from scrimmage, a new NFL record streak.

Big Leg: Oakland K **Sebastian Janikowski** now has 55 field goals of 50-plus yards, an NFL all-time best.

Good Days: New England QB **Tom Brady** now has 21 career games with at least 4 TDs and no interceptions—the most ever.

Aaron Rodgers made fantasy owners happy!

FANTASY STARS

From NFL.com's Fantasy Football game.

POS.	PLAYER, TEAM	POINTS
QB	**Aaron Rodgers**, Green Bay	380.02
RB	**David Johnson**, Arizona	327.80
WR	**Mike Evans**, Tampa Bay	208.10
TE	**Travis Kelce**, Kansas City	138.00
K	**Matt Bryant**, Atlanta	170.00
DEF	**Kansas City Chiefs**	166.00

2017 Hall of Fame

A large class of greats joined the Pro Football Hall of Fame in 2017.

Morten Andersen K
◆ Only the second kicker in the HOF ◆ All-time leader in points and field goals ◆ Played for five teams but mostly the Saints and Falcons

Terrell Davis RB
◆ Helped Broncos win two Super Bowls ◆ Ran for 2,008 yards in 1998 and won MVP

Kenny Easley S
◆ Hard-hitting safety for Seahawks ◆ Once led NFL in interceptions

Jerry Jones Owner
◆ Bought Cowboys in 1989 and helped them win three Super Bowls

Jason Taylor DE
◆ Fast and powerful sack monster for the Dolphins

LaDainian Tomlinson RB ▶
◆ Second all-time in rushing TDs ◆ Set record with 31 TDs in 2006 with the Chargers

Kurt Warner QB
◆ Two-time MVP led Rams and Cardinals to three Super Bowls total ◆ Won SB XXXIV with Rams

For the Record

Super Bowl Winners

GAME	SEASON	WINNING TEAM	LOSING TEAM	SCORE	SITE
LI	2016	**New England**	Atlanta	**34–28** (OT)	Houston
L	2015	**Denver**	Carolina	**24–10**	Santa Clara
XLIX	2014	**New England**	Seattle	**28–24**	Glendale, AZ
XLVIII	2013	**Seattle**	Denver	**43–8**	East Rutherford, NJ
XLVII	2012	**Baltimore**	San Francisco	**34–31**	New Orleans
XLVI	2011	**NY Giants**	New England	**21–17**	Indianapolis
XLV	2010	**Green Bay**	Pittsburgh	**31–25**	Arlington, TX
XLIV	2009	**New Orleans**	Indianapolis	**31–17**	Miami
XLIII	2008	**Pittsburgh**	Arizona	**27–23**	Tampa
XLII	2007	**NY Giants**	New England	**17–14**	Glendale, AZ
XLI	2006	**Indianapolis**	Chicago	**29–17**	Miami
XL	2005	**Pittsburgh**	Seattle	**21–10**	Detroit
XXXIX	2004	**New England**	Philadelphia	**24–21**	Jacksonville
XXXVIII	2003	**New England**	Carolina	**32–29**	Houston
XXXVII	2002	**Tampa Bay**	Oakland	**48–21**	San Diego
XXXVI	2001	**New England**	St. Louis	**20–17**	New Orleans
XXXV	2000	**Baltimore**	NY Giants	**34–7**	Tampa
XXXIV	1999	**St. Louis**	Tennessee	**23–16**	Atlanta
XXXIII	1998	**Denver**	Atlanta	**34–19**	Miami
XXXII	1997	**Denver**	Green Bay	**31–24**	San Diego
XXXI	1996	**Green Bay**	New England	**35–21**	New Orleans
XXX	1995	**Dallas**	Pittsburgh	**27–17**	Tempe
XXIX	1994	**San Francisco**	San Diego	**49–26**	Miami

GAME	SEASON	WINNING TEAM	LOSING TEAM	SCORE	SITE
XXVIII	1993	**Dallas**	Buffalo	**30–13**	Atlanta
XXVII	1992	**Dallas**	Buffalo	**52–17**	Pasadena
XXVI	1991	**Washington**	Buffalo	**37–24**	Minneapolis
XXV	1990	**NY Giants**	Buffalo	**20–19**	Tampa
XXIV	1989	**San Francisco**	Denver	**55–10**	New Orleans
XXIII	1988	**San Francisco**	Cincinnati	**20–16**	Miami
XXII	1987	**Washington**	Denver	**42–10**	San Diego
XXI	1986	**NY Giants**	Denver	**39–20**	Pasadena
XX	1985	**Chicago**	New England	**46–10**	New Orleans
XIX	1984	**San Francisco**	Miami	**38–16**	Stanford
XVIII	1983	**LA Raiders**	Washington	**38–9**	Tampa
XVII	1982	**Washington**	Miami	**27–17**	Pasadena
XVI	1981	**San Francisco**	Cincinnati	**26–21**	Pontiac, MI
XV	1980	**Oakland**	Philadelphia	**27–10**	New Orleans
XIV	1979	**Pittsburgh**	Los Angeles	**31–19**	Pasadena
XIII	1978	**Pittsburgh**	Dallas	**35–31**	Miami
XII	1977	**Dallas**	Denver	**27–10**	New Orleans
XI	1976	**Oakland**	Minnesota	**32–14**	Pasadena
X	1975	**Pittsburgh**	Dallas	**21–17**	Miami
IX	1974	**Pittsburgh**	Minnesota	**16–6**	New Orleans
VIII	1973	**Miami**	Minnesota	**24–7**	Houston
VII	1972	**Miami**	Washington	**14–7**	Los Angeles
VI	1971	**Dallas**	Miami	**24–3**	New Orleans
V	1970	**Baltimore**	Dallas	**16–13**	Miami
IV	1969	**Kansas City**	Minnesota	**23–7**	New Orleans
III	1968	**NY Jets**	Baltimore	**16–7**	Miami
II	1967	**Green Bay**	Oakland	**33–14**	Miami
I	1966	**Green Bay**	Kansas City	**35–10**	Los Angeles

TIGER, TIGER, BURNING BRIGHT
*No. 4 was No. 1 after Clemson's DeShaun Watson threw
a game-winning TD pass with six seconds left to beat
Alabama. The Tigers' epic 35–31 win in the national
championship game capped off a busy and record-
filled season in college football.*

COLLEGE FOOTBALL

Good Timing!

From the minute that the 2015 National Championship Game ended to the kickoff of the 2016 contest, everyone was waiting for it to happen again. In 2015, Clemson and Alabama met in an epic clash . . . and fans wanted a repeat! Throughout the 2016 season, the two schools clearly had the top teams in the land. In the end, the fans got their wish, and Clemson and 'Bama played one of the most memorable games in years. This time, Clemson got revenge and pulled out a dramatic last-second victory for its first national title in 35 years.

The 2016 season had lots of other highlights along the way. The rest of the teams weren't just watching: they wanted a playoff spot, too!

In the Big Ten, Ohio State was the early favorite, but they were stunned by Penn State, thanks to a blocked field goal. Penn State went on to win the Big Ten championship but was shut out of the College Football Playoff by Ohio State! OSU had a key win against archrival Michigan to clinch its spot. The Big Ten ended with four teams in the top 10 at the end of the season. The normally strong SEC was dominated by Alabama. Its conference-championship-game win was a sound defeat of Florida. Clemson was the talk of

2016 TOP 10

1. **Clemson**
2. **Alabama**
3. **USC**
4. **Washington**
5. **Oklahoma**
6. **Ohio State**
7. **Penn State**
8. **Florida State**
9. **Wisconsin**
10. **Michigan**

USC QB Sam Darnold

the ACC. Only a one-point loss to Pitt hurt its tremendous season. Virginia Tech gave them a run for their money in the ACC title game, but the Tigers rolled into the playoff.

Out west, USC's record fell to 1–3 early. Most people wrote the Trojans' season off. Then they rallied and won nine straight games. But Washington was given a spot in the playoffs after winning the Pac-12 title. USC did, however, take part in what turned out to be the second-best postseason game.

Western Michigan got some national attention. It entered the bowl season undefeated. They fell to No. 9 Wisconsin in the Cotton Bowl, but just making it there was a big deal for this mid-major school.

Along the way, there were amazing upsets, stunning plays, and new stars created. Read about all of it inside!

AWARD WINNERS

HEISMAN TROPHY (BEST PLAYER)
MAXWELL AWARD (PLAYER OF THE YEAR)
WALTER CAMP TROPHY (PLAYER OF THE YEAR)
Lamar Jackson/LOUISVILLE ▶▶▶

DOAK WALKER AWARD (RUNNING BACK)
D'Onta Foreman/TEXAS

DAVEY O'BRIEN AWARD (QUARTERBACK)
Deshaun Watson/CLEMSON

BILETNIKOFF AWARD (WIDE RECEIVER)
Dede Westbrook/OKLAHOMA

JOHN MACKEY AWARD (TIGHT END)
Jake Butt/MICHIGAN

OUTLAND TROPHY (INTERIOR LINEMAN)
Cam Robinson/ALABAMA

NAGURSKI TROPHY (DEFENSIVE PLAYER)
CHUCK BEDNARIK AWARD (DEFENSIVE PLAYER)
Jonathan Allen/ALABAMA

BUTKUS AWARD (LINEBACKER)
Reuben Foster/ALABAMA

JIM THORPE AWARD (DEFENSIVE BACK)
Adoree' Jackson/USC

SEASON HIGHLIGHTS

August/September

→ **Call to Arms:** Navy fourth-string QB **Malcolm Perry** started the game in his Navy uniform and ended it in a football jersey. He had been ill all week, so he sat with other students instead of dressing for the game. By halftime, the team sounded a call because of injuries to other players. Perry came out of the stands to help the Midshipmen wrap up a 52–16 win over Fordham.

→ **Surprise Scores:** Big plays handed a pair of underdogs surprise victories. Central Michigan used a hook-and-lateral play to beat No. 22 Oklahoma State. Then Houston returned a missed field goal 109 yards to help them upset No. 3 Oklahoma.

→ **Record Crowd:** Fans set a new all-time college football attendance record at a September game. But it was the venue, not the teams, that was the main attraction at this Tennessee vs. Virginia Tech matchup.

The game was played at Bristol Motor Speedway, normally the home of NASCAR races. The total of 156,990 fans squashed the old record of 115,109 set at Michigan in 2013. Of course, they can't race cars at Michigan Stadium! And the game? Tennessee won 45–24.

→ **Still an Upset?:** North Dakota State plays a division below the Bowl Championship level. But it has put together six straight "upset" wins over teams in the top division. This time, it beat No. 13 Iowa 23–21 on a last-play field goal by **Cam Pedersen**.

→ **Cardinal Stomp:** Louisville QB **Lamar Jackson** continued an amazing early-season run. He ran for 4 TDs to help his team crush No. 2 Florida State 63–20. It was one of the most lopsided defeats ever for a top-3-ranked team. Jackson then had five more TD passes and a pair of TD runs as the Cardinals beat Marshall 59–28.

College football's biggest crowd ever packed the seats at Bristol.

→ **LA Weekend:** Both of Los Angeles's big teams suffered last-minute losses. First, USC gave up a winning touchdown pass to lose to Utah with 16 seconds left. The next day, UCLA had No. 7 Stanford on the ropes. But the Cardinal scored on an 8-yard TD pass with 24 seconds left. To rub it in, they ran back a fumble for another TD as time expired.

SEASON HIGHLIGHTS
October

→ **What an Ending!:** The Georgia-Tennessee game was an instant classic. A back-and-forth battle, the game seemed over when Georgia scored with just 10 seconds left. But a penalty and a short kickoff gave Tennessee one more shot. **Joshua Dobbs** launched a Hail Mary that **Jauan Jennings** snagged amid a cluster of hands. The stunning TD gave the Volunteers a 34–31 win.

→ **Battle of Stars:** No. 5 Clemson was led by **Deshaun Watson**, who threw for 5 TDs in the game. No. 3 Louisville boasted star Lamar Jackson, who ran for a pair of scores. He led his team to the 3-yard line in the final seconds but couldn't get another score, and Clemson won 42–36.

→ **Navy Sinks Cougars:** Navy's ships rule the waves, but on this day, Navy's runners ruled the turf. The Midshipmen ran for 306 yards and upset No. 6 Houston 46–40. Navy's student body was so happy, the school canceled classes for a day to celebrate the team's first win over a top 10 team since 1984!

→ **Big Ten Showdown:** No. 2 Ohio State held onto its high national ranking with an overtime win over No. 8 Wisconsin. After the two teams tied 23–23, **J.T. Barrett** threw a game-winning TD pass in the first OT.

→ **Biggest Upset of the Year!:** No. 2 Ohio State was shocked by Penn State. The Nittany Lions scored the final 13 points of the game, including a blocked field goal

Oh, you! Mayfield set a record for OU!

returned for a TD. That gave them a 24–21 win. It was the school's first win over a No. 2 team since 1964!

→ **Super Stats!:** Stat geeks worked as hard as the players in Oklahoma's 66–59 win over Texas Tech. The teams put up a Big 12 record—1,708 total yards of offense. Tech's **Patrick Mahomes** had 819 total yards himself, a Division 1 record. Part of that total was his record-tying 734 yards of passing. OU's **Baker Mayfield** set a school record with 7 TD passes.

→ **Easy to Cheer For:** Though Pitt running back **James Conner**'s team lost to Virginia Tech, he became the second-leading runner in school history. Why is this big news? Conner had battled back to the field after fighting off cancer!

November

Samuel's score capped off a classic rivalry game.

goal with seconds left. Finally, USC beat No. 4 Washington 26–13. The upsets scrambled the playoff rankings as the season drew to a close.

➜ Welcome to the Big Ten:
Rutgers played its first season in the Big Ten, but it might regret that decision. It lost to Ohio State, Michigan, and Michigan State by a combined 185–0.

➜ Epic Upset:
Kansas fans tore down the goalposts after their team beat Texas 24–21 in overtime. It was the first win for the Jayhawks over the Longhorns since 1938! It also broke a 19-game Big 12 losing streak for Kansas.

➜ Here Come the Huskies:
When Texas A&M was named No. 4, it left undefeated Washington out. So the Huskies were a bit angry when they took on California. The Golden Bears kept it close, but only for about 15 minutes. The Huskies romped to a 66–27 victory. **Jake Browning** set a school record by throwing for 6 TDs.

➜ The Best Team You've Never Heard Of:
No. 17 Western Michigan rolled to its ninth straight win, swamping Ball State, 52–20. Their great season was somewhat hidden, however, since they play in the Mid-American Conference.

➜ Upset Saturday:
On November 12, three of the top four teams in the playoff rankings lost! Iowa thrilled its hometown fans with a 14–13 win over No. 2 Michigan, on a final-play field goal. Pittsburgh beat No. 3 Clemson 43–42, also on a field

➜ Don't Vote for Us!:
Since 1977, San Diego State has made it into the Top 25 rankings four times. Each time, the school has lost its next game. The Aztecs kept their sad streak going by losing to Wyoming 34–33.

➜ A Classic Rivalry:
Ohio State and Michigan have played each other 112 times since their first matchup in 1897. None of those games had gone to overtime (of course, OT only started in 1996). That is, not until 2016. No. 2 OSU nipped No. 3 Michigan 30–24 in overtime. The Buckeyes tied the game at 17–17 on a field goal on the last play from scrimmage. In the second overtime, Ohio State boldly went for it on fourth and one while trailing. They made it, and on the next play, **Curtis Samuel** ran 15 yards for the game-winning score.

December

CONFERENCE CHAMPIONSHIPS

ACC Clemson's all-everything **DeShaun Watson** had 3 TD passes and ran for two more scores to lead his team over Virginia Tech 42–35. Clemson needed everything Watson had, as Tech put up a stronger battle than expected. Clemson also needed a win to earn its No. 2 ranking in the national playoff.

Big Ten In one of the best games of championship weekend, Penn State rallied from 21 points down to beat Wisconsin. The Badgers came out strong and had a 28–7 lead in the first half. But the Nittany Lions scored 3 straight TDs to tie it. They took the lead for good with a fourth-quarter TD and won 38–31. They headed to the Rose Bowl on a nine-game winning streak.

SEC It was no surprise that Alabama won this game. After all, they hadn't lost all season, and this win gave them three straight SEC titles. The surprise was the winning margin. The Tide crushed the Florida State Seminoles 54–16. 'Bama scored on returns of an interception and a blocked punt.

ARMY SINKS NAVY!

The annual Army-Navy game is an American classic. The two schools pause from their work of training American military leaders to battle in football. Navy has been hot lately, winning 14 straight matchups. In 2016, Army broke through. They made several big fourth-down conversions and held on to win 21–17, sparking the Corps of Cadets to invade the field!

Pac-12 Before the season started, Colorado was picked to finish last in the Pac-12. Instead, they were one of the nation's Cinderella teams. They won seven more conference games than last season, as well as the Pac-12 South. But their glass cleats broke in this game when they were crushed by No. 4 Washington 41–10.

Penn State RB Saquon Barkley

Bowl Game Recap

The Bowl Season included a record 41 college football bowls. Here are some of the most memorable moments.

Record Runner:
The Las Vegas Bowl probably would not have been as big of a deal if not for **Donnel Pumphrey**. The San Diego State runner gained 115 yards. That gave him 6,405 for his four-year career— the all-time best at the top division of college football. San Diego State won the game, too, beating Houston 34–10.

Kick a Winner:
Louisiana Tech celebrated on the field in Fort Worth, Texas, seconds after **Jonathan Barnes** made a 32-yard field goal. That gave Tech a 48–45 win over Navy in the Armed Forces Bowl. QB **Ryan Higgins** had 4 TD passes for the Bulldogs.

All or Nothing:
In the first quarter of the Famous Idaho Potato Bowl, neither Idaho nor Colorado State scored. Then Idaho

Record-setter Donnel Pumphrey

piled up 61 points in the next three quarters, while CSU nearly matched them with 50! CSU scored an amazing 36 points in the fourth quarter alone, but it wasn't enough for the W.

Almost:
No. 8 Wisconsin ended Western Michigan's try for an undefeated season. The Badgers won the Cotton Bowl 24–16, a rare bright spot for the Big Ten, which went 3–7 in bowl games.

Happy Hurricanes:
The University of Miami used to be a college football powerhouse. From 1983 to 2001, "the U" won four titles and contended for several others. They had a solid 2016 season, though, and capped it off with their first bowl win in 10 years. The unranked Hurricanes upset No. 14 West Virginia 31–14 in the Russell Athletic Bowl in Orlando.

A Rose to Remember

The highlight of the bowl season was the Granddaddy of Them All. The 103rd playing of the Rose Bowl turned into one of the best ever.

USC came in on an eight-game winning streak after a poor start to their season. Penn State had begun the year on a down note, too, but then won nine straight. (They also just missed a spot in the College Football Playoff, finishing the regular season ranked No. 5.) One of those streaks would end, but it took the whole game to find out which.

USC jumped to a 13–0 lead in the first quarter. By the end of the half, Penn State trailed 27–21. In a TV interview on his way to the locker room, Penn State coach **James Franklin** said, "We hate the first half. Watch what we do in the second."

He was right . . . for a while. The third quarter was indeed a shocker. The Nittany Lions scored touchdowns on their first three plays from scrimmage: a 79-yard run by **Saquon Barkley**, a 72-yard catch by **Chris Godwin**, and a 3-yard run by QB **Trace McSorley** after a Penn State interception. Just like that, it was 42–27 Penn State. After USC got a score back, Penn State went back to a 14-point lead on a pass from McSorley to Barkley.

The fourth quarter was a reverse of the third. USC QB **Sam Darnold** was just about perfect. He showed calm leadership while driving the Trojans to score after score. USC scored the final 17 points of the game. Darnold would end up with 5 TD passes to

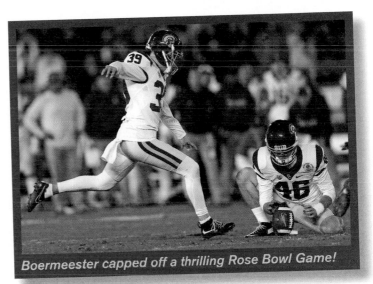

Boermeester capped off a thrilling Rose Bowl Game!

set an all-time Rose Bowl record.

After making a big interception, USC capped off their comeback when kicker **Matt Boermeester** booted a 46-yard field goal to give USC the amazing win 52–49.

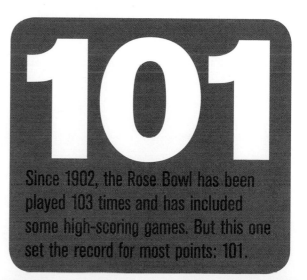

101

Since 1902, the Rose Bowl has been played 103 times and has included some high-scoring games. But this one set the record for most points: 101.

SEMIFINALS
2016 Playoffs

Alabama 24, Washington 7

The Huskies scored the first touchdown of the game . . . but then Alabama shut them down. The Crimson Tide returned to a championship game for the sixth time in eight years with a great defensive performance. They held Washington to a season low of 194 total yards (64 of which came on that first-quarter TD drive). The Crimson Tide scored yet another defensive touchdown, their 11th of the season, on a pick-six. On offense, 'Bama relied on RB **Bo Scarbrough**. He had 180 yards rushing and scored twice.

Clemson 31, Ohio State 0

For the first time in more than 190 games as a head coach, OSU's **Urban Meyer** was shut out. Clemson rolled over the Big Ten representative thanks to another great outing by QB **DeShaun Watson**. The Heisman Trophy runner-up threw a TD pass and ran for two additional scores. On defense, Clemson shut down OSU completely. They picked off two passes and held the Buckeyes to 88 yards rushing, more than 170 less than OSU's season average.

In the playoff, Washington had no answer for Scarbrough's power and speed.

2016 CHAMPIONSHIP
The Tigers Roar!

Clemson 35, Alabama 31

With six seconds left in the National Championship Game, **Deshaun Watson** and Clemson were staring history in the face. They had lost to Alabama in this game a year earlier. The Crimson Tide was going for its fifth title in eight years. Clemson had not won in 35 years. From the two-yard line, could Clemson punch in a score to snatch away the trophy?

Watson got the snap, rolled right, and hit **Hunter Renfrow** with a perfect pass. Touchdown! *Championship!*

That was the capper to a thrilling game. Alabama's powerful defense kept Clemson bottled up most of the night. They led 14–7 at the half thanks to two scores by power runner **Bo Scarbrough**. However, Scarbrough went out in the third quarter with a knee injury. A TD pass from Watson to Renfrow brought Clemson to within three points. That seemed to give the Tigers new life. Then 'Bama struck back with a 68-yard TD pass from **Jalen Hurts** to tight end **O.J. Howard**.

That led to a wild fourth quarter. Clemson opened with a Watson-to-**Mike Williams** TD pass. The two teams swapped punt after punt before a wild final five minutes.

After a long drive, Clemson's **Wayne Gallman** dove in for a score that gave Clemson

Watson proudly holds the trophy.

its first lead of the game. However, Hurts soon scored on a twisting 30-yard run that put Alabama ahead with just over two minutes left. Could Watson drive through the great Tide D?

He could.

Williams, Renfrow, and **Jordan Leggett** made amazing clutch catches on the drive. A pass-interference call put the ball on the two and set up the winning score.

As confetti rained down on the field, a new champion of college football was crowned!

We're No. 1!

These are the teams that have finished at the top of the Associated Press's final rankings since the poll was first introduced in 1936.

SEASON	TEAM	RECORD	SEASON	TEAM	RECORD
2016	Clemson	14-1	1975	Oklahoma	11-1
2015	Alabama	14-1	1974	Oklahoma	11-0
2014	Ohio State	14-1	1973	Notre Dame	11-0
2013	Florida State	14-0	1972	USC	12-0
2012	Alabama	13-1	1971	Nebraska	13-0
2011	Alabama	12-1	1970	Nebraska	11-0-1
2010	Auburn	14-0	1969	Texas	11-0
2009	Alabama	14-0	1968	Ohio State	10-0
2008	Florida	13-1	1967	USC	10-1
2007	LSU	12-2	1966	Notre Dame	9-0-1
2006	Florida	13-1	1965	Alabama	9-1-1
2005	Texas	13-0	1964	Alabama	10-1
2004	USC	13-0	1963	Texas	11-0
2003	USC	12-1	1962	USC	11-0
2002	Ohio State	14-0	1961	Alabama	11-0
2001	Miami (FL)	12-0	1960	Minnesota	8-2
2000	Oklahoma	13-0	1959	Syracuse	11-0
1999	Florida State	12-0	1958	LSU	11-0
1998	Tennessee	13-0	1957	Auburn	10-0
1997	Michigan	12-0	1956	Oklahoma	10-0
1996	Florida	12-1	1955	Oklahoma	11-0
1995	Nebraska	12-0	1954	Ohio State	10-0
1994	Nebraska	13-0	1953	Maryland	10-1
1993	Florida State	12-1	1952	Michigan State	9-0
1992	Alabama	13-0	1951	Tennessee	10-1
1991	Miami (FL)	12-0	1950	Oklahoma	10-1
1990	Colorado	11-1-1	1949	Notre Dame	10-0
1989	Miami (FL)	11-1	1948	Michigan	9-0
1988	Notre Dame	12-0	1947	Notre Dame	9-0
1987	Miami (FL)	12-0	1946	Notre Dame	8-0-1
1986	Penn State	12-0	1945	Army	9-0
1985	Oklahoma	11-1	1944	Army	9-0
1984	Brigham Young	13-0	1943	Notre Dame	9-1
1983	Miami (FL)	11-1	1942	Ohio State	9-1
1982	Penn State	11-1	1941	Minnesota	8-0
1981	Clemson	12-0	1940	Minnesota	8-0
1980	Georgia	12-0	1939	Texas A&M	11-0
1979	Alabama	12-0	1938	Texas Christian	11-0
1978	Alabama	11-1	1937	Pittsburgh	9-0-1
1977	Notre Dame	11-1	1936	Minnesota	7-1
1976	Pittsburgh	12-0			

NATIONAL CHAMPIONSHIP GAMES

Until the 2014 season, there was no national championship playoff system at the highest level of college football. From 1998 to 2013, the NCAA ran the Bowl Championship Series, which used computers and polls to come up with a final game that pitted the No. 1 team against the No. 2 team. The new system, called the College Football Playoff, has a panel of experts that sets up a pair of semifinal games to determine which teams play for the national title. Here are the results of BCS and College Football Playoff finals since 2000.

SEASON	TEAMS AND SCORE	SITE
2016	**Clemson 35, Alabama 31**	TAMPA, FL
2015	**Alabama 45, Clemson 40**	GLENDALE, AZ
2014	**Ohio State 42, Oregon 20**	ARLINGTON, TX
2013	**Florida State 34, Auburn 31**	PASADENA, CA
2012	**Alabama 42, Notre Dame 14**	MIAMI, FL
2011	**Alabama 21, LSU 0**	NEW ORLEANS, LA
2010	**Auburn 22, Oregon 19**	GLENDALE, AZ
2009	**Alabama 37, Texas 21**	PASADENA, CA
2008	**Florida 24, Oklahoma 14**	MIAMI, FL
2007	**LSU 38, Ohio State 24**	NEW ORLEANS, LA
2006	**Florida 41, Ohio State 14**	GLENDALE, AZ
2005	**Texas 41, USC 38**	PASADENA, CA
2004	**USC 55, Oklahoma 19**	MIAMI, FL
2003	**LSU 21, Oklahoma 14**	NEW ORLEANS, LA
2002	**Ohio State 31, Miami (FL) 24 (2 OT)**	TEMPE, AZ
2001	**Miami (FL) 37, Nebraska 14**	PASADENA, CA
2000	**Oklahoma 13, Florida State 2**	MIAMI, FL

MLB

WHAT A WIN!

The Chicago Cubs won their first World Series in 108 years! The city turned its river Cubs blue as five million people celebrated. Chicago's amazing season was capped by one of the most thrilling Game 7s in baseball history. Relive all the incredible details on page 59.

Smile, Cubs!

One of the best things about baseball is how it connects us to the past. The game is new each year, with new players and new ways of playing. There's new gear and new stadiums. But all are connected to the game that's been a part of America for more than 150 years.

In 2016, that connection between the past and present was on every fan's mind. Why? The Chicago Cubs entered the season favored by many experts to win the title. But they not only hadn't won the World Series since 1908, but they hadn't even made it to one since 1945! As the Cubbies rolled through the year–they ended with the best record in 2016–history seemed ready to come alive.

Meanwhile, other teams with long histories of missing out on a championship were chasing their own dreams. The Texas Rangers have never won a World Series. (That includes their 11 seasons as the Washington Senators before moving to the Lone Star State in 1972.)

The Cleveland Indians' last championship came in 1948, and they've only won twice since they started in 1901! Then there were the Washington Nationals, another team expected to be a contender in 2016. They started as the Montreal Expos in 1969 and still don't have a World Series win. Compared to those teams, the Los Angeles Dodgers had nothing to complain about. Their championship-free streak only goes back to 1988!

All these teams were chasing history in 2016. Some of them got pretty close, but only one ended up making it.

The Texas Rangers used power pitching from **Yu Darvish** and **Cole Hamels** to rack up the American League's most wins. The Nationals had the NL's second-best record, thanks to help from slugging second baseman **Daniel Murphy**. The Los Angeles Dodgers had more players on the disabled list and used more pitchers in one season than any other team in history. Somehow, they still won 91 games and made the playoffs.

Indians manager **Terry Francona** had already led Boston to a pair of World

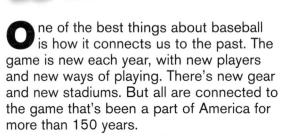

Murphy led the NL with a .595 slugging average.

PAPI POWER

Boston designated hitter **David "Big Papi" Ortiz** hung up his oversized spikes after the 2016 season. He was one of the most popular and beloved players in the game. He helped the Red Sox win the World Series in 2004, 2007, and 2013. Along the way, he set all-time DH records with 1,761 hits and 485 home runs. (His career total of 541 homers puts him 17th among all players.) Big Papi saved his best for last, winning the Hank Aaron Award as the AL's top offensive player. His 127 RBI led the AL and were the most ever for a player in his final season. He also led the league in doubles and slugging average. Adios, Big Papi!

Series wins. He found the magic again in Cleveland. His team used speed and a deep bullpen to power through the season and the playoffs.

There were other teams in the mix. The Toronto Blue Jays waited until the final day of the regular season to clinch a playoff spot. So did the San Francisco Giants, who also earned a wild-card berth. In that same game, announcer **Vin Scully**—the voice of the Dodgers—called his last game after an amazing 67 years." Now that's a guy who has seen a lot of baseball history—but even he was not around to see the last time a season ended like this one did.

The World Series came down to the Cubs and Indians, each of whom would make history if they won. As it turned out, they played a super-memorable Series. Read all about it starting on page 58. It was one for the history books!

2016 FINAL STANDINGS

AL EAST		AL CENTRAL		AL WEST	
Red Sox*	93–69	Indians*	94–67	Rangers*	95–67
Blue Jays*	89–73	Tigers	86–75	Mariners	86–76
Orioles*	89–73	Royals	81–81	Astros	84–78
Yankees	84–78	White Sox	78–84	Angels	74–88
Rays	68–94	Twins	59–103	Athletics	69–93

NL EAST		NL CENTRAL		NL WEST	
Nationals*	95–67	Cubs*	103–58	Dodgers*	91–71
Mets*	87–75	Cardinals	86–76	Giants*	87–75
Marlins	79–82	Pirates	78–83	Rockies	75–87
Phillies	71–91	Brewers	73–89	Diamondbacks	69–93
Braves	68–93	Reds	68–94	Padres	68–94

*Playoff teams

MLB Playoffs!

ALDS

Blue Jays 3, Rangers 0

Toronto blasted an ALDS-record 8 homers and swept Texas. The Blue Jays won the clincher 7–6 in 10 innings when **Josh Donaldson** motored home to score on an error as the Rangers tried to turn an inning-ending double play. It was the first postseason series in Major League history decided by an error on the final play.

Indians 3, Red Sox 0

Cleveland matched the Blue Jays with a sweep of Boston. Star Red Sox pitchers **David Price** and **Rick Porcello** could not tame Cleveland's powerful bats. The series marked the end of the awesome career of Boston DH **David "Big Papi" Ortiz**, who retired following the last game. Boston fans saluted him as he teared up on the mound.

On to the ALCS! Toronto's Josh Donaldson leaps up after scoring the ALDS winning run.

NLDS
Cubs 3, Giants 1
It looked like the Giants would force a Game 5 in their series against the Cubs. But Chicago set a postseason record by coming from three runs behind in the ninth inning of Game 4. They scored four runs to win the game 6–5 and the series three games to one.

Dodgers 3, Nationals 2
In the only LDS that went five games, the Dodgers outlasted the Nationals. In the deciding Game 5, LA manager **Dave Roberts** skillfully used his pitching staff. The key was the work of closer **Kenley Jansen**. Roberts brought him in early, in the seventh inning. To shut the door in the ninth inning of a 4–3 victory, Roberts called on starter **Clayton Kershaw**, who had already won two games in the series and had pitched just two days earlier. It was a gutsy pitching performance and sent the Dodgers to the NLCS.

ALCS
Indians 4, Blue Jays 1
This series was a blowout, but not in the way most people thought it would be. Cleveland won the first two games in Toronto and never looked back. The

WILD CARD GAMES
Madison Bumgarner did it again for the Giants. One of the best postseason pitchers ever threw nine shutout innings against the Mets. Third baseman **Conor Gillaspie** hit a three-run homer in the ninth inning for the only runs in the Giants' 3–0 victory. In the AL, **Edwin Encarnacion** had his own three-run bomb. It came in the bottom of the 11th, giving the Blue Jays a 5–2 walk-off win over the Orioles.

Indians' deep pitching staff shut down Toronto's bats. In the Indians' four wins, they allowed the Blue Jays only three runs. Relief ace **Andrew Miller** was the MVP after pitching in four games. He allowed no runs and struck out 14 batters in 7.2 innings. Cleveland earned its first trip to the World Series since 1997.

NLCS
Cubs 4, Dodgers 2
After waiting 71 years, Cubs fans would finally get to see their beloved team in the World Series. The Cubbies won the last three games while outscoring LA 23–6. In the clinching sixth game, starter **Kyle Hendricks** and closer **Aroldis Chapman** faced the minimum 27 batters—only the second time that has ever happened in a postseason game.

2016 World Series

One thing was for sure when the 2016 World Series started—one team would break a *loooong* streak. The Indians had not won a World Series since 1948. The Cubs had not won since 1908. Those were the two longest championship droughts in the sport!

GAME 1
Indians 6, Cubs 0

Cleveland ace **Corey Kluber** made the Cubs look like they left their bats in Chicago. He set a World Series record with 8 strikeouts in his first three innings. Catcher **Roberto Pérez** backed up his pitcher with a pair of home runs.

GAME 2
Cubs 5, Indians 1

Chicago ace **Jake Arrieta** pulled a Kluber and shut down Cleveland. He was helped by a pair of RBI from DH **Kyle Schwarber**, who had missed nearly the full regular season because of a knee injury. His amazing recovery inspired the Cubs, who tied the series as it headed for Chicago.

GAME 3
Indians 1, Cubs 0

This was a surprising pitchers' duel in the first World Series game at Wrigley Field since 1945. **Coco Crisp** drove in the game's only run. Cleveland's bullpen silenced the Cubs' powerful offense.

GAME 4
Indians 7, Cubs 2

Cleveland shocked Cubs fans by winning again in Chicago. Kluber shut down the Cubs a second time. **Jason Kipnis** had 3 RBI to put the Indians one win away from the title.

GAME 5
Cubs 3, Indians 2

In a must-win game, the Cubs came through. Chicago closer **Aroldis Chapman** nailed down the final eight outs to protect a one-run lead. Chicago got all its runs in the fourth inning, highlighted by **Kris Bryant**'s homer.

GAME 6
Cubs 9, Indians 3

This one was over early, as the Cubs scored three in the first inning. Arrieta was great, and Chapman got some key outs, too. Chicago's **Addison Russell** tied a World Series record with 6 RBI in the game, including a grand slam. After a long season, it would all come down to a fateful Game 7.

Kluber notched two wins for the Indians.

Cubs Win Thrilling Game 7

Cubs 8, Indians 7

When you tell your grandkids you saw this game, they'll be amazed. In the long history of the World Series (it started in 1903!), this was one of the most thrilling and nail-biting games ever. The game was played in Cleveland, but the Cubs seemed to have, as one reporter wrote, a "road-field advantage." Chicago came in very hot, having won two straight games. But it was do-or-die for both teams. One of the biggest TV audiences in decades watched, while every seat in Cleveland was filled (including some by celebrities such as **LeBron James**!).

Indians fans were shocked when **Dexter Fowler** led off the game with a homer for the Cubs. Cleveland tied it in the third on a **Carlos Santana** single. Chicago added a pair of runs in the fourth, then a **Javier Báez** homer in the fifth. **Anthony Rizzo** then lined an RBI single off **Andrew Miller**, who had been unhittable until that point. The Indians trailed 5–1, but in the bottom of the inning, they scored two runs on one wild pitch!

Chicago catcher **David Ross**, playing his last game at age 39, hit a homer in the sixth to make the score 6–3. Cubs fans were ready to celebrate in Chicago!

With a man on and two outs in the eighth, the Cubs brought in fireballing **Aroldis Chapman**. The first batter, **Brandon Guyer**, lined a run-scoring double. Then **Rajai Davis** rocked the night with a game-tying two-run homer!

Neither team scored in the ninth, but then Mother Nature called a time-out. A rain delay let the Cubs regroup. In the tenth, they rallied. **Kyle Schwarber**

As Rizzo snagged the ball . . . Cubs WIN!

got his seventh hit of the Series. Pinch-runner **Albert Almora** then scored on a double by **Ben Zobrist** (later named World Series MVP). **Miguel Montero** drove in Rizzo, who had walked. The Cubs led 8–6 and were three outs from breaking a 108-year-old curse.

The Indians made it interesting, though. Davis drove in another run. But **Mike Montgomery**, the Cubs' fifth pitcher, earned his first big-league save by retiring **Michael Martinez** on a grounder. As third baseman **Kris Bryant** fired the ball to first, he had a huge smile on his face.

It was the smile of a champion!

2016 Awards

MOST VALUABLE PLAYER

AL: **Mike Trout**
ANGELS

NL: **Kris Bryant**
CUBS

CY YOUNG AWARD

AL: **Rick Porcello**
RED SOX

NL: **Max Scherzer**
NATIONALS

Porcello won 22 games for the Red Sox.

ROOKIE OF THE YEAR

AL: **Michael Fulmer**
TIGERS

NL: **Corey Seager**
DODGERS

MANAGER OF THE YEAR

AL: **Terry Francona**
INDIANS

NL: **Dave Roberts**
DODGERS

HANK AARON AWARD

AL: **David Ortiz**
RED SOX

NL: **Kris Bryant**
CUBS

ROBERTO CLEMENTE AWARD
(FOR COMMUNITY SERVICE)

Curtis Granderson
METS

4

Kris Bryant was the first player to win four straight player of the year awards. He won in college in 2013, earned minor league top honors in 2014, and was the NL Rookie of the Year in 2015.

Stat Leaders

NL Hitting Leaders

.348 BATTING AVERAGE
DJ LeMahieu, Rockies

41 HOME RUNS
Nolan Arenado, Rockies
Chris Carter, Brewers

133 RBI
Nolan Arenado, Rockies

62 STOLEN BASES
Jonathan Villar, Brewers

AL Hitting Leaders

.338 BATTING AVERAGE
José Altuve, Astros

47 HOME RUNS
Mark Trumbo, Orioles

127 RBI
Edwin Encarnacion, Blue Jays
David Ortiz, Red Sox

43 STOLEN BASES
Rajai Davis, Indians

Arenado had 40-plus HRs for a second season.

NL Pitching Leaders

20 WINS
Max Scherzer, Nationals

284 STRIKEOUTS
Max Scherzer, Nationals

2.13 ERA
Kyle Hendricks, Cubs

51 SAVES
Jeurys Familia, Mets

AL Pitching Leaders

22 WINS
Rick Porcello, Red Sox

254 STRIKEOUTS
Justin Verlander, Tigers

3.00 ERA
Aaron Sanchez, Blue Jays

47 SAVES
Zach Britton, Orioles

Around the Bases 2016

Weird Way to Reach Base:

Yankees outfielder **Jacoby Ellsbury** has some speed, can hit homers, and plays a fine center field. But he has one special talent that sets him apart. In 2016, he reached base reaching base on catcher's interference 11 times, setting a new MLB record for a single season. That also made him second all-time in this painful stat with 25 total in his career.

Tough Call:

Dodgers manager **Dave Roberts** made a difficult decision in a September game. His pitcher, **Rich Hill**, had not allowed a base runner to the Marlins. In other words, he was working on a perfect game. Such a game has been pitched only 24 other times in baseball history! But you have to finish the game. The Dodgers led 5–0 after seven innings, but Roberts was worried about making a blister on Hill's hand worse. So he made the sad choice. It was the latest that a player has ever been taken out in such a situation.

Running Out of K Cards:

In a game in September, Boston pitchers set an MLB record with 23 strikeouts in a 3–2 victory against the Rays in 10 innings. Starter **Eduardo Rodriguez** led the way with 13 strikeouts. Four relievers added the rest. They set another record, too: 11 straight strikeouts from the fourth to seventh, by Rodriguez and **Heath Hembree**.

Sad Day:

Marlins ace pitcher **José Fernández** and two friends were killed when their boat crashed into rocks in Miami Beach, Florida. All of baseball mourned the 24-year-old star's death. Fernández was admired for his talent and outgoing personality. He was also known for the dangerous road he had traveled from Cuba to make it to the Majors. The Marlins played a game shortly after while all wearing his No. 16 jersey.

◀◀◀Second Base Power:

Twins 2B **Brian Dozier** smacked 42 homers, the most ever for an AL player at his position.

Baseball Goes to the Dogs

The Chicago White Sox did something no other team did. They set a new world record during Bark at the Park. On that day, 1,122 dogs attended the game with their "partners." The folks from Guinness World Records were on hand to make it official!

ALL OR NOTHING

Players are going for the fences . . . or not. This chart shows how both home runs have been rising steadily. But so have strikeouts. In 2016, teams combined to set a record for strikeouts (38,982) for the 11th straight season! Plus, the 5,610 total homers (shown here) were the second most of all time!

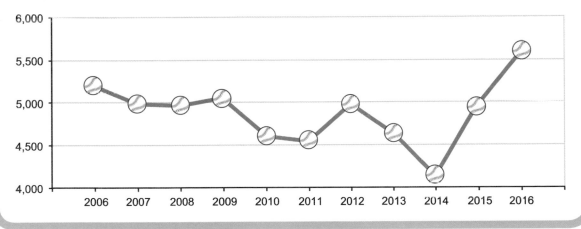

A New Bronx Bomber?

Yankees catcher **Gary Sanchez** certainly made his mark when he joined the team for good on August 3, 2016. He hit a homer in his sixth game . . . and didn't stop! Sanchez clubbed 19 homers in his first 45 Major League games. That was the most ever to start a career. He ended with 20 in his 53 games. Sanchez wasn't the only impressive hitter this season. In 2016, 103 other players also hit 20 or more home runs, setting an all-time MLB record.

Around the Bases 2017

Mmm, Crunchy!: Seattle served up one of the most unique ballpark treats ever. The Mariners offered their fans a serving of toasted grasshoppers! The crunchy insects were such a hit the first time the team had them on the menu that the Mariners had to order twice as many for the next homestand!

Good Day in DC: Washington third baseman **Anthony Rendon** had a day for the record books against the Mets on April

3,343

That's how many homers big leaguers slugged before the 2017 All-Star Game break. That's the most ever to this point in the season. Fans in the bleachers, watch out!

30. He slugged 3 homers and drove in 10 runs while going six-for-six at the plate. That combination of batting feats had not been accomplished in a game since 1949. Thanks in large part to Rendon, the Nats won 23–5.

◄◄◄García Times Three: For the first time, a team started an outfield that had all three players sharing the same last name: **García**. When the Chicago White Sox took the field against Minnesota on April 14, **Willy** was in left, **Leury** in center, and **Avisail** in right. None of them are related, either!

Here Comes the Judge: At 25, Yankees OF **Aaron Judge** became the youngest player with 13 homers in his team's first 26 games. And they weren't just regular homers—the 6' 7" rookie averaged more than 400 feet on those massive blasts! (For more on Judge, see page TK.)

Scooter's Big Day: When you've hit 38 home runs in 1,637 at-bats, you don't expect to hit four in a single game. But that's what Cincinnati's **Scooter Gennett** did when his team routed St. Louis 13–1 on June

6. He became the first MLB player ever with 5 hits, including 4 homers, and 10 RBI in one game. The Hall of Fame collected his jersey for display after his historic night.

◀◀◀A Grand Day in Baseball:

On June 3, seven grand slams were hit in the Majors. That's the most "grand salamis" in one day in big-league history! The highlight was one smacked by the Angels' **Albert Pujols**. It was his 600th career homer! He became the ninth player to reach that amazing total but the first to do so by clearing the bases with one swing!

Mr. Everything: Houston's **Marwin Gonzalez** has to double check the lineup carefully. In the first month of the 2017 season, he played first, second, and third bases, along with left field . . . and hit a homer while playing in each position! That gave the versatile veteran an all-time MLB first.

US Beats the World

Baseball is called "America's National Pastime." But the US had never won the World Baseball Classic, which features national teams from around the world. That finally changed in March 2017 when the Americans knocked off Puerto Rico 8–0 in the championship game at Dodger Stadium in Los Angeles. Starting pitcher **Marcus Stroman** pitches for the Toronto Blue Jays, but he grew up in New York state. He threw six scoreless innings to earn game MVP honors. **Ian Kinsler** blasted a two-run homer to get the scoring started. **Brandon Crawford** added a two-run single later. **David Robertson** closed out the game, and the US had its first WBC trophy.

World Series Winners

YEAR	WINNER	RUNNER-UP	SCORE*	YEAR	WINNER	RUNNER-UP	SCORE*
2016	Chicago Cubs	Cleveland Indians	4-3	1989	Oakland Athletics	San Francisco Giants	4-0
2015	Kansas City Royals	New York Mets	4-1	1988	Los Angeles Dodgers	Oakland Athletics	4-1
2014	San Francisco Giants	Kansas City Royals	4-3	1987	Minnesota Twins	St. Louis Cardinals	4-3
2013	Boston Red Sox	St. Louis Cardinals	4-2	1986	New York Mets	Boston Red Sox	4-3
2012	San Francisco Giants	Detroit Tigers	4-0	1985	Kansas City Royals	St. Louis Cardinals	4-3
2011	St. Louis Cardinals	Texas Rangers	4-3	1984	Detroit Tigers	San Diego Padres	4-1
2010	San Francisco Giants	Texas Rangers	4-1	1983	Baltimore Orioles	Philadelphia Phillies	4-1
2009	New York Yankees	Philadelphia Phillies	4-2	1982	St. Louis Cardinals	Milwaukee Brewers	4-3
2008	Philadelphia Phillies	Tampa Bay Rays	4-1	1981	Los Angeles Dodgers	New York Yankees	4-2
2007	Boston Red Sox	Colorado Rockies	4-0	1980	Philadelphia Phillies	Kansas City Royals	4-2
2006	St. Louis Cardinals	Detroit Tigers	4-1	1979	Pittsburgh Pirates	Baltimore Orioles	4-3
2005	Chicago White Sox	Houston Astros	4-0	1978	New York Yankees	Los Angeles Dodgers	4-2
2004	Boston Red Sox	St. Louis Cardinals	4-0	1977	New York Yankees	Los Angeles Dodgers	4-2
2003	Florida Marlins	New York Yankees	4-2	1976	Cincinnati Reds	New York Yankees	4-0
2002	Anaheim Angels	San Francisco Giants	4-3	1975	Cincinnati Reds	Boston Red Sox	4-3
2001	Arizona Diamondbacks	New York Yankees	4-3	1974	Oakland Athletics	Los Angeles Dodgers	4-1
2000	New York Yankees	New York Mets	4-1	1973	Oakland Athletics	New York Mets	4-3
1999	New York Yankees	Atlanta Braves	4-0	1972	Oakland Athletics	Cincinnati Reds	4-3
1998	New York Yankees	San Diego Padres	4-0	1971	Pittsburgh Pirates	Baltimore Orioles	4-3
1997	Florida Marlins	Cleveland Indians	4-3	1970	Baltimore Orioles	Cincinnati Reds	4-1
1996	New York Yankees	Atlanta Braves	4-2	1969	New York Mets	Baltimore Orioles	4-1
1995	Atlanta Braves	Cleveland Indians	4-2	1968	Detroit Tigers	St. Louis Cardinals	4-3
1993	Toronto Blue Jays	Philadelphia Phillies	4-2	1967	St. Louis Cardinals	Boston Red Sox	4-3
1992	Toronto Blue Jays	Atlanta Braves	4-2	1966	Baltimore Orioles	Los Angeles Dodgers	4-0
1991	Minnesota Twins	Atlanta Braves	4-3	1965	Los Angeles Dodgers	Minnesota Twins	4-3
1990	Cincinnati Reds	Oakland Athletics	4-0	1964	St. Louis Cardinals	New York Yankees	4-3

* Score is represented in games played.

YEAR	WINNER	RUNNER-UP	SCORE*	YEAR	WINNER	RUNNER-UP	SCORE*
1963	Los Angeles Dodgers	New York Yankees	4-0	1933	New York Giants	Washington Senators	4-1
1962	New York Yankees	San Francisco Giants	4-3	1932	New York Yankees	Chicago Cubs	4-0
1961	New York Yankees	Cincinnati Reds	4-1	1931	St. Louis Cardinals	Philadelphia Athletics	4-3
1960	Pittsburgh Pirates	New York Yankees	4-3	1930	Philadelphia Athletics	St. Louis Cardinals	4-2
1959	Los Angeles Dodgers	Chicago White Sox	4-2	1929	Philadelphia Athletics	Chicago Cubs	4-1
1958	New York Yankees	Milwaukee Braves	4-3	1928	New York Yankees	St. Louis Cardinals	4-0
1957	Milwaukee Braves	New York Yankees	4-3	1927	New York Yankees	Pittsburgh Pirates	4-0
1956	New York Yankees	Brooklyn Dodgers	4-3	1926	St. Louis Cardinals	New York Yankees	4-3
1955	Brooklyn Dodgers	New York Yankees	4-3	1925	Pittsburgh Pirates	Washington Senators	4-3
1954	New York Giants	Cleveland Indians	4-0	1924	Washington Senators	New York Giants	4-3
1953	New York Yankees	Brooklyn Dodgers	4-2	1923	New York Yankees	New York Giants	4-2
1952	New York Yankees	Brooklyn Dodgers	4-3	1922	New York Giants	New York Yankees	4-0
1951	New York Yankees	New York Giants	4-2	1921	New York Giants	New York Yankees	5-3
1950	New York Yankees	Philadelphia Phillies	4-0	1920	Cleveland Indians	Brooklyn Robins	5-2
1949	New York Yankees	Brooklyn Dodgers	4-1	1919	Cincinnati Reds	Chicago White Sox	5-3
1948	Cleveland Indians	Boston Braves	4-2	1918	Boston Red Sox	Chicago Cubs	4-2
1947	New York Yankees	Brooklyn Dodgers	4-3	1917	Chicago White Sox	New York Giants	4-2
1946	St. Louis Cardinals	Boston Red Sox	4-3	1916	Boston Red Sox	Brooklyn Robins	4-1
1945	Detroit Tigers	Chicago Cubs	4-3	1915	Boston Red Sox	Philadelphia Phillies	4-1
1944	St. Louis Cardinals	St. Louis Browns	4-2	1914	Boston Braves	Philadelphia Athletics	4-0
1943	New York Yankees	St. Louis Cardinals	4-1	1913	Philadelphia Athletics	New York Giants	4-1
1942	St. Louis Cardinals	New York Yankees	4-1	1912	Boston Red Sox	New York Giants	4-3
1941	New York Yankees	Brooklyn Dodgers	4-1	1911	Philadelphia Athletics	New York Giants	4-2
1940	Cincinnati Reds	Detroit Tigers	4-3	1910	Philadelphia Athletics	Chicago Cubs	4-1
1939	New York Yankees	Cincinnati Reds	4-0	1909	Pittsburgh Pirates	Detroit Tigers	4-3
1938	New York Yankees	Chicago Cubs	4-0	1908	Chicago Cubs	Detroit Tigers	4-1
1937	New York Yankees	New York Giants	4-1	1907	Chicago Cubs	Detroit Tigers	4-0
1936	New York Yankees	New York Giants	4-2	1906	Chicago White Sox	Chicago Cubs	4-2
1935	Detroit Tigers	Chicago Cubs	4-2	1905	New York Giants	Philadelphia Athletics	4-1
1934	St. Louis Cardinals	Detroit Tigers	4-3	1903	Boston Americans	Pittsburgh Pirates	5-3

Note: 1904 not played because NL-champion Giants refused to play; 1994 not played due to MLB work stoppage.

THE END OF THE STREAK

Mississippi State's Morgan William launched this jumper against Connecticut in a national semifinal. When William came down, the ball went in, and the buzzer went off. Winner! Mississippi State won, shocking the sports world and ending Connecticut's NCAA-record 111-game winning streak.

COLLEGE BASKETBALL

Epic Endings

End of a Streak

Until the second-to-last game of the year, the big story in women's college hoops was Connecticut. Would the Huskies ever lose? They came into the season with a 75-game winning streak and having won the past four NCAA titles. Their first target was to beat their own record streak of 90 consecutive wins, set from 2008 to 2010. They flew by that number in January, winning their 91st straight with a romp over SMU. Now fans wondered, how high could they go?

Meanwhile, the other big story in women's hoops was whether Kelsey Plum would break the all-time scoring record. The Washington senior poured in points all year, but began her last regular-season game needing a few more to break the record. With the help of her teammates, she scored a career single-game high 57 points in a win over Utah. She ended with a career total 3,397 points—four more than Jackie Stiles's old record.

While Plum and her Huskies didn't make the Final Four, Connecticut did . . . and that's when its remarkable run came to an end with an upset by Mississippi State. Read more on page 77.

Someone Had to Win

The men's 2016–17 season featured so many story lines, fans needed a chart to keep track! Several teams pushed to the top of the pack as the season went on, but none really stood out until the final game.

Gonzaga had never made it to the Final Four; could it take that final step? Kentucky once again included a cast of amazing freshmen, led by high-scoring Malik Monk. Kansas, helped by superstar Frank Mason III, rose to the No. 1 spot late in the regular season. From the West, a trio of Pac-12 teams—UCLA, Oregon, and Arizona—roared into the national picture. The Bruins were led by future NBA star Lonzo Ball. But Oregon used a powerful inside game to win the Pac-12 championship.

Defending champion Villanova was in the mix, but it could not repeat its 2016 miracle. Finally, there was, as always, North Carolina. The veteran team was steady and successful. Was that the way to reach the top? Find out on page 75.

Plum was a peach while setting a new scoring record.

MAJOR AWARDS

Two players swept the three major awards in men's and women's college hoops.

NAISMITH AWARD
JOHN R. WOODEN AWARD
AP PLAYER OF THE YEAR

Frank Mason III/KANSAS ▶
Kelsey Plum/WASHINGTON

AP COACH OF THE YEAR
MEN'S
Mark Few/GONZAGA
WOMEN'S
Geno Auriemma/CONNECTICUT

FINAL MEN'S TOP 10
USA Today Coaches Poll

1. North Carolina
2. Gonzaga
3. Oregon
4. Kansas
5. Kentucky
6. South Carolina
7. Arizona
8. Villanova
9. UCLA
10. Florida

FINAL WOMEN'S TOP 10
USA Today Coaches Poll

1. South Carolina
2. Mississippi State
3. Connecticut
4. Stanford
5. Notre Dame
6. Baylor
7. Florida State
8. Maryland
9. Oregon State
10. Ohio State

2016-17 Highlights

the way" in California means many hoops fans don't get to see how good they are. That changed in December when UCLA upset powerful Kentucky. The Bruins moved from No. 11 to No. 2 in the polls!

◀◀◀ THE BUTLER DID IT:

At 14-0, Villanova was ranked No. 1 and hoping to repeat its NCAA title. But in a January regular-season game, surprising Butler pulled off a major upset. The Bulldogs beat the Wildcats 66-58. And proving it was no fluke, they won again in February when Villanova was ranked No. 2!

DOWN UNDER THUNDER:

St. Mary's is a small school in Moraga, California. But the Gaels found themselves in the national rankings thanks in part to some imports. They had seven players from Australia on their team, led by top scorer Jock Landale. Those players helped St. Mary's win 28 regular-season games and earn a spot in the NCAA Tournament.

EARLY THRILLER: Unranked Kentucky beat No. 7 North Carolina 103-100 in a matchup of famous hoops schools. Malik Monk set a Wildcats freshman record with 47 points in the high-scoring showdown. His three-pointer put the Wildcats up late, and they held on for the win.

HERE COME THE BRUINS!: UCLA fans often say that their team doesn't get the attention it deserves. They say that playing "all

SHORT STAY: Baylor's women's team has been a national force for a while. In January 2017, Baylor's men's team got some love, too. The Bears earned the No. 1 ranking for the first time in school history. In their first game as No. 1, though, they became No. 1 in another category: most turnovers in school history (29). They lost 89–68 to No. 10 West Virginia, which meant the Bears wouldn't be No. 1 the next week!

Central Michigan's Marcus Keene averaged 30 points per game to lead the nation in scoring. He topped 40 points in a game seven times, with a high of 50.

the game was in Kansas! The Jayhawks had won 51 games in a row on their home court before the Cyclones beat them 92–89.

BIG UPSET: The rankings on January 30 put the Gonzaga Bulldogs in the No. 1 spot for just the second time in school history. They enjoyed the top spot for a month before their first loss of the season on February 25. BYU pulled off one of the biggest upsets of the year, winning 79–71.

LATE MAGIC: Down by 14 points with just over a minute to play? No problem—at least not if you're Nevada. The Wolfpack trailed New Mexico 90–76 with 74 seconds left. In a wild sequence that featured six straight three-pointers, Nevada stormed back to tie the game. Then in overtime, the Wolfpack squeaked out a surprising 105–104 win.

WESTERN SHOWDOWN: For the first time in 10 seasons, two top five Pac-12 teams squared off when No. 5 UCLA played at No. 4 Arizona. UCLA held on for a big victory 77–72. It was its third win of the season over a top-five team.

RANKINGS SHAKEUP: On January 24, the Nos. 1, 2, and 4 teams all lost! Villanova fell to Marquette, Kansas was swarmed by West Virginia, and Kentucky lost a squeaker to Tennessee. It was the first time since 1979 that three teams ranked that high lost on the same night!

FINALLY DANCING: After 78 years of trying to make it to NCAA Tournament play, Northwestern earned its first visit to the Big Dance. The Wildcats edged Michigan 67–65 on a buzzer-beater to assure themselves of a spot.

HOME COOKIN' GOES SOUR: Iowa State beat Kansas in February. It was an upset, but what really made news is that

NCAA Tournament

The 2017 NCAA Tournament had fewer big early-round upsets than usual. But there were still some memorable games on the way to the Final Four.

Gophers Struck: No. 12-seed Middle Tennessee pulled off the biggest upset of the first round, defeating No. 5 Minnesota. The Golden Gophers had been a surprise entry. They were making their first trip to the tournament since 2013 and just their fifth this century. But it was a short stay as the Blue Raiders won 81–72.

X Marks the Ws: No. 11-seed Xavier made it the farthest of any high seed. The Musketeers beat No. 6 Maryland and then No. 3 Florida State—wiping out the Seminoles 91–66!—to make the Sweet 16. They then upset No. 2 Arizona before losing to top-seeded Gonzaga!

USC Takes Two: No. 11-seed USC had to win a "First Four" game, coming back from 17 points down against Providence, to earn its spot in the final 64 teams. Then it came back again, trailing by 10 points before squeaking out a 66–65 win over No. 6 SMU.

Best Game?: There were many close games in the rounds before the Final Four, but one stood out for drama and big plays. No. 8-seed Wisconsin trailed No. 4 Florida by 12 points late in the second half, but came back to tie and force overtime. The two teams battled back and forth and the score stayed tight. Nigel Hayes made two free throws with four seconds left. That seemed to seal the deal. The Gators could not stop the clock, so Chris Chiozza dribbled across midcourt and popped a long three-point shot. As the buzzer went off, the ball went through the net. Florida celebrated its 84–83 comeback victory.

Michigan's players battled adversity.

◀◀◀ Feel-Good Story: The Michigan Wolverines were the inspirational story of the first weekend. Before the Big Ten Tournament, the airplane on which they were flying skidded off a runway while landing. The near-miss shook up the players, but they rebounded with a shocking run to win that tournament. The seventh-seeded Wolverines then beat No. 10 Oklahoma State and upset No. 2 Louisville to make a surprising Sweet 16 appearance.

THE FINAL FOUR
North Carolina 77, Oregon 76

Oregon beat surprising Michigan to make the Final Four for the first time since the NCAA Tournament began in 1939. North Carolina rode in as a No. 1-seed and nearly gave the game away. With a one-point lead after a hard-fought back-and-forth game, North Carolina kept missing free throws. But Oregon kept missing rebounds. In the final seconds, the Tar Heels missed four from the stripe but got the ball back each time. It was a golden opportunity for the Ducks, but they could not come through.

The Tar Heels celebrated the school's sixth national title.

Gonzaga 77, South Carolina 73

Gonzaga was playing in its 19th consecutive NCAA Tournament and had reached the Final Four for the first time. South Carolina was the Cinderella team—a No. 7 seed that crushed No. 3 Baylor to make the national semifinal. But the Gamecocks ran out of magic dust in this game, though the outstanding **Sindarius Thornwell** did his best. South Carolina made just two buckets in the final seven minutes, and Gonzaga headed to the title game for the first time in its history.

CHAMPIONSHIP
North Carolina 71, Gonzaga 65

Gonzaga was making its first appearance ever in the Final Four. North Carolina was enjoying its 20th. Sure, none of its players had been there 20 times, but the experience of the program and the people around it showed. The game was sloppy, with far too many fouls, but North Carolina remained calm. Though many fans hoped for underdog Gonzaga to win, the Tar Heels—led by guard **Joel Berry II**—prevailed. It was sweet revenge for North Carolina, which had lost the 2016 title game on a buzzer-beater by Villanova.

NCAA Women's Hoops

The women's NCAA tournament rarely sees many early-round upsets. Still, there were some highlights worth noting on the way to the Final Four.

Hooray for Quinnipiac!: The surprise win by No. 12-seed Quinnipiac over No. 5 Marquette gave hope to tiny schools everywhere. With just 8,000 students, the "Q" is not quite an athletic giant. But they had enough to beat a very solid Marquette team 68–65. It was the school's first-ever win in the NCAA Tournament. But it gets better. The team then shocked No. 4 Miami (FL) to reach the Sweet 16!

Ducks Quack!: Oregon's men's team made the Final Four, and the women's team nearly matched that feat. Though seeded No. 10, the Ducks upset No. 7 Temple, No. 3 Maryland, and No. 2 Duke before falling to the UConn powerhouse.

Big Margins: Several early-round games showed the divide between really great schools and merely good ones. South Carolina beat UNC Asheville 90–40. Duke smashed Hampton 94–31. Connecticut steamrollered Albany by 61 points, 116–55. Baylor topped even those lopsided margins, crushing Texas Southern 119–30. Women's hoops has a long way to go to become better balanced.

Big Comeback: There were some pretty good matchups in the later rounds, but one stood out. No. 2 Stanford had to rally from 16 points behind to defeat Notre Dame 76–75. It was a fierce battle between two top programs. A late block by Erica McCall clinched the Cardinal's win.

Stanford rose above Notre Dame.

WOMEN'S TOURNAMENT

End of the Streak!

Connecticut headed into its semifinal against Mississippi State having won 111 games in a row. This one ended with the smallest player on the court making the biggest shot. The game was close throughout, as the Bulldogs stayed step-for-step with the four-time defending champs. The second half ended with the score tied at 60. In overtime, UConn had a chance to win, but lost the ball. That gave 5' 5" **Morgan William** a chance to make history. She buried a buzzer-beating 14-footer—and the Huskies' record-setting streak was over! In the other semifinal, South Carolina continued its great tournament run with an easy win over Stanford.

A New Champion!

With UConn out, women's college hoops was guaranteed to have a new champion for the first time since 2012. The shock of beating the Huskies must have taken some of the steam out of Mississippi State. The Bulldogs had trouble scoring, and star guard William could manage only 8 points. Still, their defense kept it close. South Carolina led by only four points before the Gamecocks' star forward **A'ja Wilson** (left) took over. The tournament's Most Outstanding Player had 8 points, 3 rebounds, and 2 blocks in the final minutes to clinch the championship 67–55. It was the school's first-ever national basketball title.

NCAA Champs!

MEN'S DIVISION I

2017 North Carolina	1998 Kentucky	1979 Michigan State
2016 Villanova	1997 Arizona	1978 Kentucky
2015 Duke	1996 Kentucky	1977 Marquette
2014 Connecticut	1995 UCLA	1976 Indiana
2013 Louisville	1994 Arkansas	1975 UCLA
2012 Kentucky	1993 North Carolina	1974 NC State
2011 Connecticut	1992 Duke	1973 UCLA
2010 Duke	1991 Duke	1972 UCLA
2009 North Carolina	1990 UNLV	1971 UCLA
2008 Kansas	1989 Michigan	1970 UCLA
2007 Florida	1988 Kansas	1969 UCLA
2006 Florida	1987 Indiana	1968 UCLA
2005 North Carolina	1986 Louisville	1967 UCLA
2004 Connecticut	1985 Villanova	1966 Texas Western
2003 Syracuse	1984 Georgetown	1965 UCLA
2002 Maryland	1983 NC State	1964 UCLA
2001 Duke	1982 North Carolina	1963 Loyola (Illinois)
2000 Michigan State	1981 Indiana	1962 Cincinnati
1999 Connecticut	1980 Louisville	1961 Cincinnati

1960 **Ohio State**	1952 **Kansas**	1944 **Utah**
1959 **California**	1951 **Kentucky**	1943 **Wyoming**
1958 **Kentucky**	1950 **City Coll. of NY**	1942 **Stanford**
1957 **North Carolina**	1949 **Kentucky**	1941 **Wisconsin**
1956 **San Francisco**	1948 **Kentucky**	1940 **Indiana**
1955 **San Francisco**	1947 **Holy Cross**	1939 **Oregon**
1954 **La Salle**	1946 **Oklahoma A&M**	
1953 **Indiana**	1945 **Oklahoma A&M**	

WOMEN'S DIVISION I

2017 **South Carolina**	2005 **Baylor**	1993 **Texas Tech**
2016 **Connecticut**	2004 **Connecticut**	1992 **Stanford**
2015 **Connecticut**	2003 **Connecticut**	1991 **Tennessee**
2014 **Connecticut**	2002 **Connecticut**	1990 **Stanford**
2013 **Connecticut**	2001 **Notre Dame**	1989 **Tennessee**
2012 **Baylor**	2000 **Connecticut**	1988 **Louisiana Tech**
2011 **Texas A&M**	1999 **Purdue**	1987 **Tennessee**
2010 **Connecticut**	1998 **Tennessee**	1986 **Texas**
2009 **Connecticut**	1997 **Tennessee**	1985 **Old Dominion**
2008 **Tennessee**	1996 **Tennessee**	1984 **USC**
2007 **Tennessee**	1995 **Connecticut**	1983 **USC**
2006 **Maryland**	1994 **North Carolina**	1982 **Louisiana Tech**

A RING FOR KD
Kevin Durant slams home a shot during the 2017 NBA Finals. KD had joined the Golden State Warriors with one goal: cap his super career with a championship. Consider that goal reached. KD led the Warriors to the title over the Cleveland Cavaliers.

2016-17 Season

After battling through 13 playoff games over two years, the score between the Warriors and Cavaliers was 1–1. Huh? Well, in games, Golden State had won 7 and Cleveland had won 6. But each team had won one NBA title by beating the other. In 2015, the Warriors rolled to their first title since 1975. In 2016, the Cavs staged a miracle comeback to win their first NBA championship ever.

As the 2016–17 season rolled on, a third NBA Finals clash seemed like destiny. It would be a first. The same two teams had never met in the Finals three times in a row. Would they make history?

The other 28 teams had something to say about that, of course. However, it was soon clear that Cleveland and Golden State were far above the competition. They did have a couple of teams nipping at their heels. About halfway through the season, four teams had fewer than 10 losses. The Cavs and Warriors were two of them, and they were joined by the always-tough San Antonio Spurs and the fast-rising Houston Rockets.

The Rockets were led by all-around star James "The Beard" Harden. Always a star, he had his best season yet, leading the NBA in assists and finishing second in points scored. The Spurs depended on **Kawhi Leonard**. Once known mostly for his defense, he has emerged as a full-court star. He earned All-NBA honors for the second consecutive season.

Other teams that had positive seasons include the Washington Wizards, led by **John Wall**, and the LA Clippers, sparked by **Chris Paul**. The Toronto Raptors won as many games as the Cavaliers, thanks in part to high-scoring guard **DeMar DeRozan**.

Meanwhile, one player was earning more headlines by himself than most entire teams. Oklahoma City guard **Russell Westbrook** was challenging one of the NBA's oldest records. In 1961–62, the great **Oscar Robertson** put up 41 triple-

Fear the Beard! Houston's James Harden

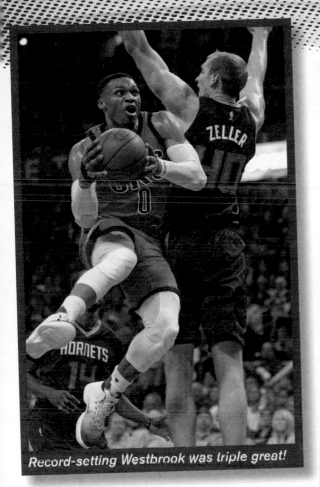

Record-setting Westbrook was triple great!

doubles—reaching double digits in three stat categories in one game—for the Cincinnati Royals. (The Royals are now the Sacramento Kings.) In Westbrook's first eight seasons, he had a total of 37 such games. Right out of the box, Westbrook set his sights on Robertson's record. He put together two streaks of seven straight. In March, he had a triple-double while not missing a single shot. Westbrook ended with 42 triple-doubles to top Robertson. To cap it all off, Westbrook averaged a triple-double for the season. No one had done that since Robertson, either!

After the regular season, everyone watched the playoffs, waiting for the NBA Finals that some people called the "Thrillogy"! Read what happened on page 85.

2016–2017 FINAL STANDINGS

EASTERN CONFERENCE

ATLANTIC DIVISION	W–L
Celtics	53–29
Raptors	51–31
Knicks	31–51
76ers	28–54
Nets	20–62

CENTRAL DIVISION	W–L
Cavaliers	51–31
Bucks	42–40
Pacers	42–40
Bulls	41–41
Pistons	37–45

SOUTHEAST DIVISION	W–L
Wizards	49–33
Hawks	43–39
Heat	41–41
Hornets	36–46
Magic	29–53

WESTERN CONFERENCE

NORTHWEST DIVISION	W–L
Jazz	51–31
Thunder	47–35
Trail Blazers	41–41
Nuggets	40–42
Timberwolves	31–51

PACIFIC DIVISION	W–L
Warriors	67–15
Clippers	51–31
Kings	32–50
Lakers	26–56
Suns	24–58

SOUTHWEST DIVISION	W–L
Spurs	61–21
Rockets	55–27
Grizzlies	43–39
Pelicans	34–48
Mavericks	33–49

2017 NBA Playoffs

From the start, the Warriors and Cavs looked so dominant, the playoffs were a race for third and fourth place. Here are some highlights from the rounds before the NBA Finals.

Thomas led the Celts to the Conference Finals.

Not Even with Westbrook:

The NBA's triple-double twins, **Russell Westbrook** and **James Harden**, faced off in the first round. Harden's Houston team proved to have more weapons, though. He averaged 33.2 points as the Rockets won in five games. Westbrook averaged 37.4 points, including a 51-point effort in Game 2, but he couldn't do it alone.

Wizards Nearly Magic:
In the conference semifinal round, **John Wall**, Washington's hot-shooting guard, buried a game-winning three-point basket late in Game 6 versus the Celtics. That forced a Game 7, but it was in Boston. The Celts used home-court magic to win the series and earn a trip to the Eastern Conference Finals.

Spurs Undone:
In the Western Conference Finals, the Warriors caught a big break. San Antonio superstar **Kawhi Leonard** went out in the first game with an ankle injury. **Stephen Curry** & Co. took full advantage and swept the Spurs.

First-Round Nail-Biter:
The Clippers and Jazz played the only seven-game series of the first round. Los Angeles had more firepower on paper, thanks to **Chris Paul** and **Blake Griffin**. However, Utah played better all around. The Jazz won Game 7 in Los Angeles, but then were swept by the Warriors in the second round.

Cleveland Rocks:
Like the Spurs, the Celtics lost their top player when **Isaiah Thomas** went down in the second game of the Eastern Conference Finals. That made it easier for **LeBron James** and Cleveland to win in five games and roar into the NBA Finals.

2017 NBA Finals

The 2017 NBA Finals featured all kinds of firsts. It was the first time that a team entered the Finals with a perfect postseason record. (The Warriors were 12–0.) It was the first time that the same two teams met in the Finals three seasons in a row. And **LeBron James** became the first player ever to average a triple-double for the entire Finals series.

But even The King was not enough to overcome the Warriors' dominant offense. The addition of **Kevin Durant** to an already-great team made Golden State just about unstoppable. Durant scored at least 30 points in each of the five games. Add in the sharpshooting of **Stephen Curry** and **Klay Thompson** and the pounding defense of **Draymond Green**, and Golden State had all the answers.

Durant poured in 38 points as Golden State won Game 1 by 22 points. The Warriors dominated in Game 2 as well, winning by 19.

The series moved to Cleveland, and the Cavaliers seemed to have Game 3 in hand late in the second half. However, the Warriors went on an 11–0 run to end the game. Durant scored the go-ahead basket with a huge three-point shot over James.

The Cavaliers did break the Warriors' playoff winning streak at 15 games with a Game 4 victory. Cleveland set an all-time Finals record with 49 points in the opening quarter and never looked back. The Cavs romped to a 137–116 win, led by **Kyrie Irving**'s 40 points.

In Game 5, however, dreams of a second straight Finals comeback ended early. Though James poured in 41 points, they were not enough to overcome the Warriors' weapons. Durant had 39 points and Curry added 34, which included 12 free throws. Golden State thrilled its home fans while earning its second NBA title in three seasons with a nine-point win.

Durant capped off his dream season by being named the NBA Finals MVP. One of the first people he found was his mom, who had been in his corner from day one. "We did it!" they shouted at each other. You sure did, KD!

Curry soared over LeBron to win it all.

NBA Awards

MR. TRIPLE-DOUBLE!

From the start of the 2016–17 season, **Russell Westbrook** was a triple-double machine. He broke a 55-year-old NBA record with 42 triple-doubles in a season. He was the first player since **Oscar Robertson** in 1961–62 to average a triple-double (points, assists, and rebounds). Westbrook also led the NBA in scoring average.

Put it all together and the choice for Most Valuable Player was easy: Westbrook in a runaway! Westbrook became the first player in Thunder franchise history to win the award. The Thunder used to be the Seattle SuperSonics, and no Seattle player was ever MVP, either.

NBA AWARDS

DEFENSIVE PLAYER OF THE YEAR	**Draymond GREEN**, Warriors
ROOKIE OF THE YEAR	**Malcolm BROGDON**, Bucks
SIXTH MAN	**Eric GORDON**, Rockets
MOST IMPROVED	**Giannis ANTETOKOUNMPO**, Bucks
SPORTSMANSHIP	**Kemba WALKER**, Hornets
COACH OF THE YEAR	**Mike D'ANTONI**, Rockets

NBA Stat Leaders

Most NBA stats are ranked "per game" (pg). The numbers below represent the average each player had for all his games in 2016–17.

31.6 POINTS (PPG)
Russell Westbrook, Thunder

11.2 ASSISTS (APG)
James Harden, Rockets

2.0 STEALS (SPG)
Draymond Green, Warriors

71.4 FIELD-GOAL PCT.
DeAndre Jordan, Clippers ▶▶▶

2,356 & 907 & 659

Those were the points, assists, and rebounds totals for Houston's Mr. All-Around, **James Harden**. He became the first player in NBA history to top 2,000 points, 900 assists, and 600 rebounds in the same season!

14.1 REBOUNDS (RPG)
Hassan Whiteside, Heat

2.6 BLOCKS (BPG)
Rudy Gobert, Jazz

45.1 3-POINT PCT.
Kyle Korver, Cavaliers

In the Paint

Great Starts:

Toronto guard **DeMar DeRozan** averaged 34.1 points in the season's first eight games, the fourth-highest start to a season ever. Oklahoma City guard **Russell Westbrook** also got off to a hot start. In his team's second game, he scored 51 points while recording a triple-double. That would be the start of a trend for Westbrook, who went on to set a new season record with 42 triple-doubles.

No Layups Here!:

Houston spent most of its game against the Pelicans in December outside the three-point arc. The Rockets set several NBA records

while winning the game 122–100. They poured in an all-time best 24 "treys" while also setting new marks for three-point attempts in a half (31) and a game (61). It was actually the second time they had beaten the game attempts record in 2016!

Best Game Ever?:

If **James Harden**'s feats in Houston's December win over the Knicks aren't the best, they are darned close. The bearded sharpshooter poured in 53 points, while dishing out 17 assists and grabbing 16 boards. ESPN reported that was the first time in NBA history that a player had topped 50/15/15 in a single game!

◀◀◀ Three-Quarter Time:

In just three quarters of a game against the Pacers in December, the Warriors' **Klay Thompson** poured in a career-high 60 points! He played less than 30 minutes overall. That made him the first player since 1954 with that many points in so few minutes! Golden State was so far ahead, Klay got the last quarter off!

A Season of 50s:

In January, Chicago guard **Jimmy Butler** scored 52 points in a win over the Hornets. He became the eighth player with a 50-point game in the 2016–17 season. That tied a record for a season, which was broken when Phoenix's **Devin Booker** poured in 70 points against the Celtics in a game in March. By the end of the year, a record 10 players had a total of 16 50-point games.

Record-Setting All-Star Game

Anthony Davis of the New Orleans Pelicans enjoyed home cooking when the All-Star Game came to his team's town. The young forward set a new record with 52 points in the (as usual) defense-free game. The teams combined for two more records: most points (374) and most dunks (75). The West "won" 192–182, but the real winners were fans who got to watch this basketball track meet!

Revenge: In January, the Warriors got a chance for some revenge against Cleveland, which had upset them in last season's NBA Finals. Golden State was on fire, and swamped the Cavs 126–91.

Another Kind of Triple-Double:

Most of these stats stories happen when players reach double digits in points, assists, and rebounds. In a February win over Memphis, Golden State forward **Draymond Green** added a new wrinkle. He had 12 rebounds, 10 assists, and 10 steals! It was the first triple-double ever without a player scoring at least 10 points.

Booker in the Record Book: ▶▶▶

Devin Booker set an all-time team record for the Phoenix Suns by pouring in 70 points in a game against the Celtics in March 2017. No other Suns player scored more than 11 points that night! At 20, Booker was the youngest player ever to reach 70, too. All his points, however, were not enough, and Boston won the game.

2016 WNBA

Taurasi claimed the career points crown.

Happy 20th birthday, WNBA! The most successful women's pro sports league in the United States celebrated its second decade in 2016 with another marvelous season of great stars and clutch performances.

As part of the celebration, the league named its top 20 players of all time. Among them: Phoenix guard **Diana Taurasi**, who in 2017 became the league's all-time leading scorer.

Another highlight for fans was watching former Connecticut star **Breanna Stewart** join the league. She was the number-one overall draft pick by the Seattle Storm after leading her Huskies to four consecutive NCAA titles. She ended up second in the league in rebounds and helped Seattle reach the playoffs.

As the season began, the defending-champion Minnesota Lynx picked up where they left off. The team set a WNBA record with 12 straight wins to start the season. The Los Angeles Sparks were one behind at 11. That marked the first time in American pro sports history—women's or men's—that two teams had started that well. Those two teams stayed strong, easily the class of the league.

The WNBA playoffs were held in a new format in 2016. During the season, the teams were divided by conference. But for the postseason, overall winning percentage determined who played whom. The bottom four seeds played each other in a single-elimination first round. The winners there were joined by the third and fourth seeds in another single-elimination round. Then those winners advanced to play the top two seeds in best-of-five series.

2016 AWARDS WINNERS

MVP: Nneka Ogwumike, Sparks
ROOKIE OF THE YEAR: Breanna Stewart, Storm
DEFENSIVE PLAYER OF THE YEAR: Sylvia Fowles, Lynx
MOST IMPROVED PLAYER: Elizabeth Williams, Dream

2016 WNBA FINALS

GAME 1: Sparks 78, Lynx 76
Showing that it takes everyone to win the big games, **Alana Beard** scored only 4 points, but two of them came at the buzzer, giving LA a crucial win.

GAME 2: Lynx 79, Sparks 60
You can't keep an MVP down for long. Minnesota star **Maya Moore** led the way in this series-tying win, scoring 21 points and grabbing 12 rebounds. Minnesota's defense shut down the high-powered Sparks, limiting them to 33-percent shooting.

GAME 3: Sparks 92, Lynx 75
When you're the league MVP, you need to show up at crunch time. **Nneka Ogwumike** poured in 21 points, while fellow superstar **Candace Parker** had 24. They led LA to a key win, putting the Sparks one win away from the title. They shut down a second-half rally by Minnesota to clinch the win.

GAME 4: Lynx 85, Sparks 79
With a chance to win the title at home, the Sparks fizzled. Moore stepped up again, putting in a series-high 31 points while

Ogwumike "sparked" LA's team!

grabbing 9 rebounds. Minnesota's defense mostly shut down LA's high-powered attack. The two teams headed back to Minnesota for a final showdown in Game 5.

GAME 5: Sparks 77, Lynx 76
The WNBA's website called this game an "instant classic." With the title on the line, both teams stepped up their game. The defense on both sides was fierce, but each also boasted top-scoring stars. With such a tight match, you'd expect it to come to the last shot . . . and it did. Moore put Minnesota ahead, but there were still 15 seconds left for the Sparks. Proving her season MVP status, Nneka Ogwumike buried a short jumper with 3.1 seconds left after snagging a rebound. That gave the Sparks their first title since 2002.

2016 WNBA FINAL STANDINGS

EASTERN CONFERENCE		WESTERN CONFERENCE	
New York	21–13	Minnesota	28–6
Chicago	18–16	Los Angeles	26–8
Indiana	17–17	Seattle	16–18
Atlanta	14–20	Phoenix	16–18
Connecticut	14–20	Dallas	11–23
Washington	13–21	San Antonio	7–27

Stat Stuff

NBA CHAMPIONS

2016-17 **Golden State**	2001-02 **LA Lakers**	1986-87 **LA Lakers**
2015-16 **Cleveland**	2000-01 **LA Lakers**	1985-86 **Boston**
2014-15 **Golden State**	1999-00 **LA Lakers**	1984-85 **LA Lakers**
2013-14 **San Antonio**	1998-99 **San Antonio**	1983-84 **Boston**
2012-13 **Miami**	1997-98 **Chicago**	1982-83 **Philadelphia**
2011-12 **Miami**	1996-97 **Chicago**	1981-82 **LA Lakers**
2010-11 **Dallas**	1995-96 **Chicago**	1980-81 **Boston**
2009-10 **LA Lakers**	1994-95 **Houston**	1979-80 **LA Lakers**
2008-09 **LA Lakers**	1993-94 **Houston**	1978-79 **Seattle**
2007-08 **Boston**	1992-93 **Chicago**	1977-78 **Washington**
2006-07 **San Antonio**	1991-92 **Chicago**	1976-77 **Portland**
2005-06 **Miami**	1990-91 **Chicago**	1975-76 **Boston**
2004-05 **San Antonio**	1989-90 **Detroit**	1974-75 **Golden State**
2003-04 **Detroit**	1988-89 **Detroit**	1973-74 **Boston**
2002-03 **San Antonio**	1987-88 **LA Lakers**	1972-73 **New York**

1971–72 **LA Lakers**	1954–55 **Syracuse**	1949–50 **Minneapolis**
1970–71 **Milwaukee**	1953–54 **Minneapolis**	1948–49 **Minneapolis**
1969–70 **New York**	1952–53 **Minneapolis**	1947–48 **Baltimore**
1968–69 **Boston**	1951–52 **Minneapolis**	1946–47 **Philadelphia**
1967–68 **Boston**	1950–51 **Rochester**	
1966–67 **Philadelphia**		
1965–66 **Boston**		

WNBA CHAMPIONS

1964–65 **Boston**	2016 **Los Angeles**	2006 **Detroit**
1963–64 **Boston**	2015 **Minnesota**	2005 **Sacramento**
1962–63 **Boston**	2014 **Phoenix**	2004 **Seattle**
1961–62 **Boston**	2013 **Minnesota**	2003 **Detroit**
1960–61 **Boston**	2012 **Indiana**	2002 **Los Angeles**
1959–60 **Boston**	2011 **Minnesota**	2001 **Los Angeles**
1958–59 **Boston**	2010 **Seattle**	2000 **Houston**
1957–58 **St. Louis**	2009 **Phoenix**	1999 **Houston**
1956–57 **Boston**	2008 **Detroit**	1998 **Houston**
1955–56 **Philadelphia**	2007 **Phoenix**	1997 **Houston**

NHL

SID THE KID!

The great Sidney Crosby brought the Stanley Cup home to the fans in Pittsburgh—again. He led the Penguins as they beat the Nashville Predators in six games in the 2017 Stanley Cup Final. The Pens became the first back-to-back Stanley Cup champs since the 1997 and 1998 Detroit Red Wings.

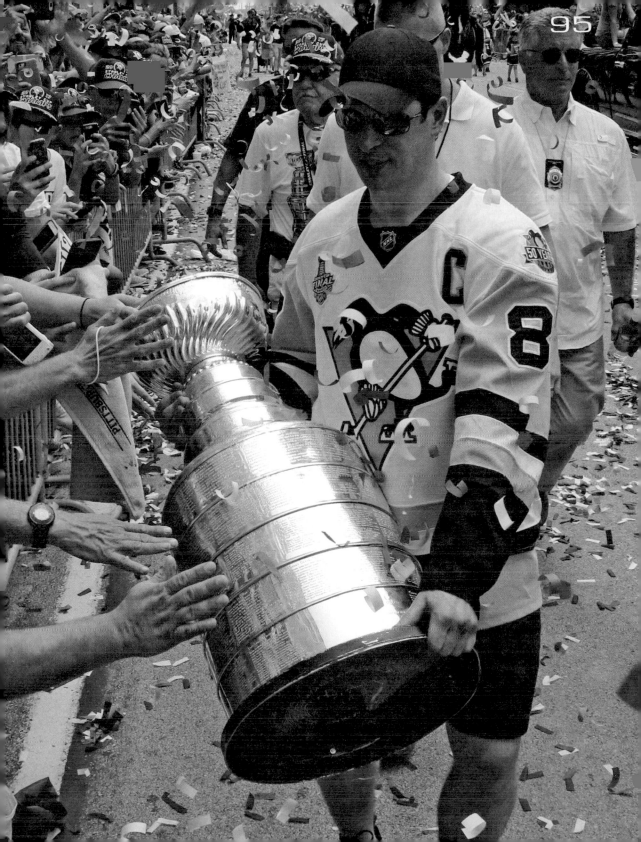

NHL Old and New!

The 2016–17 NHL season was packed with action, highlighted by some things old and some things new! The Chicago Blackhawks finished as the best in the West again, led by the dynamic duo of **Patrick Kane** and **Jonathan Toews**. But the big story of the regular season came out of Alberta, as the Edmonton Oilers had their best finish since 1987. Goalie **Cam Talbot** put up a 42-win season, and newly appointed captain **Connor McDavid** scored 100 points, leading the Oilers to a 103-point season. After an up-and-down season in which they struggled to find their game, the Nashville Predators settled into the playoffs as the final seed in the West. In July of 2016, the Predators had made headlines when they swapped their captain, **Shea Weber**, to the Montreal Canadiens for **P. K. Subban**. Subban played a huge role in his new team's success.

In the East, the usual teams—the Pittsburgh Penguins, New York Rangers, and Montreal Canadiens—all had strong finishes, but there were some newcomers as well. The Columbus Blue Jackets were the big surprise there, led by their Vezina Trophy–winning goalie, **Sergei Bobrovsky**. The Toronto Maple Leafs were another surprise, turning in their best season since 2004. Leading one of the youngest teams in hockey, head coach **Mike Babcock** guided young guns such as **William Nylander**, **Mitch Marner**, and **Auston Matthews** to a 95-point season.

In fact, it was a season in which the teens took over. Every year there's a hot young prospect everyone is talking about. Some make it big in the NHL and some don't. But the recent crop of "youngstars" really delivered. Matthews, chosen first overall in 2016, proved that growing up in sunny Arizona doesn't mean

Auston Matthews was the NHL's top rookie.

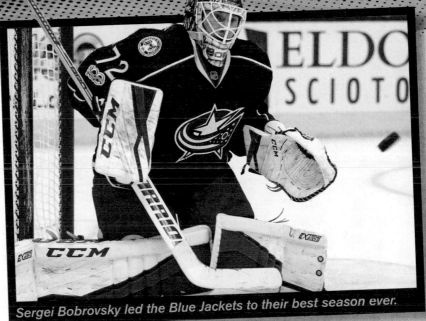

> **"Our players relax in front of 'Bob.' They see him back there, playing solid and confident. I thought he was really sharp."**
>
> — COLUMBUS COACH **JOHN TORTORELLA** ON HIS GOALIE, **SERGEI BOBROVSKY**

Sergei Bobrovsky led the Blue Jackets to their best season ever.

you can't play great hockey. He became the only player in NHL history to score 4 goals in his first game, and he ended up with 40 goals for the regular season. Other teenagers with big seasons included Connor McDavid in Edmonton, **Patrik Laine** of the Winnipeg Jets, **Noah Hanifin** and **Sebastian Aho** of the Carolina Hurricanes, **Zach Werenski** of the Columbus Blue Jackets, and **Ivan Provorov** and **Travis Konecny** of the Philadelphia Flyers.

In the end, the Washington Capitals again reigned supreme, turning in a 118-point season to win their second straight Presidents' Trophy as regular-season champs.

In the Stanley Cup playoffs, however, another team rose above them all—again.

2016-2017 NHL FINAL STANDINGS

EASTERN CONFERENCE

ATLANTIC DIVISION	PTS	METROPOLITAN DIV.	PTS
Montreal	103	Washington	118
Ottawa	98	Pittsburgh	111
Boston	95	Columbus	108
Toronto	95	NY Rangers	102
Tampa Bay	94	NY Islanders	94
Florida	81	Philadelphia	88
Detroit	79	Carolina	87
Buffalo	78	New Jersey	70

WESTERN CONFERENCE

CENTRAL DIVISION	PTS	PACIFIC DIVISION	PTS
Chicago	109	Anaheim	105
Minnesota	106	Edmonton	103
St. Louis	99	San Jose	99
Nashville	94	Calgary	94
Winnipeg	87	Los Angeles	86
Dallas	79	Arizona	70
Colorado	48	Vancouver	69

Stanley Cup Playoffs

Here are some highlights from the puck-smashing, hard-checking NHL playoffs.

Anaheim's Ryan Getzlaf celebrates!

ROUND 1

◎ The Washington Capitals had the league's best regular-season record, but they were tested in their series against the Toronto Maple Leafs. The Leafs were in the playoffs for the second time in 13 years. Five of the six games went to overtime, including the Capitals' win in Game 6.

◎ The Nashville Predators were the lowest-ranked playoff team in the league. The Chicago Blackhawks were No. 1. Predators goalie **Pekka Rinne** allowed only three goals in the entire series, and the Preds stunned the Blackhawks, eliminating them in a four-game sweep.

ROUND 2

◎ The defending-champion Pittsburgh Penguins faced the Washington Capitals for the second consecutive year. The Penguins took a 3–1 series lead, but the Capitals charged back for a Game 7 showdown. In the final game, goalie **Marc-Andre Fleury** posted a shutout as Pittsburgh moved to the next round.

◎ The Anaheim Ducks and Edmonton Oilers series was thrilling. The Oilers led 3–0 in Game 5 until **Ryan Getzlaf** scored the first of three Ducks' goals in the final 3:16 of the third period. Anaheim won in double overtime. The Ducks' **Nick Ritchie** scored the series-winning goal in Game 7.

ROUND 3

◎ The Ottawa Senators were the surprise team of the playoffs when they squared off against the mighty Penguins. Ottawa took the champs to a winner-take-all Game 7. It was a classic that went two overtime periods before the Penguins' **Chris Kunitz** scored the game winner to put his team in the Stanley Cup Final.

◎ The Predators met the Ducks in the Western Conference final. The teams split the first four games before the Predators grabbed the series lead in front of their wildly enthusiastic fans. Predators forward **Colton Sissons** scored a hat trick in Game 6, paving the way for Nashville to take the series.

Stanley Cup Final

GAME 1: Penguins 5, Predators 3

Nashville's **P. K. Subban** appeared to open the scoring in Game 1. But the goal was waved off thanks to a controversial offsides call on **Filip Forsberg**. Soon after, the Penguins scored three times in just over four minutes.

GAME 2: Penguins 4, Predators 1

After a 1–1 first period, the Predators shelled Penguins goaltender **Matt Murray**, outshooting the Penguins 14–7 over the next 20 minutes. But Murray turned them all aside, and his teammates scored three goals in the final period.

GAME 3: Predators 5, Penguins 1

In the first Stanley Cup Final game ever played in Nashville, things looked bad for the Predators when Pittsburgh scored early in the first period. In the second period, **Roman Josi** tied the game on a power play, then Nashville got two more goals to go ahead 3–1. They pulled away for the win.

GAME 4: Predators 4, Penguins 1

Calle Jarnkrok opened the scoring for Nashville late in the first period. Then Pittsburgh's **Sidney Crosby** tied it on a breakaway about a minute later. Pittsburgh didn't score in the final two periods, but the Predators put up three to tie the series.

GAME 5: Penguins 6, Predators 0

Pittsburgh fans were feeling uneasy heading into the pivotal Game 5. They didn't need to. Pittsburgh dominated and posted the first shutout of the series.

GAME 6: Penguins 2, Predators 0

The home team had not lost a game in this series, so Nashville fans expected a win. In the first period, Predators forward **Colton Sissons** appeared to tap in the puck after Murray gave up a rebound. However, in one of the most controversial moments in Stanley Cup Final history, the goal was waved off. The referee had blown his whistle before the shot. The game remained scoreless until former Predator **Patric Hornqvist** scored a goal with 1:35 remaining in the final period. The Penguins added an empty-net goal in the final seconds and won their second consecutive Stanley Cup.

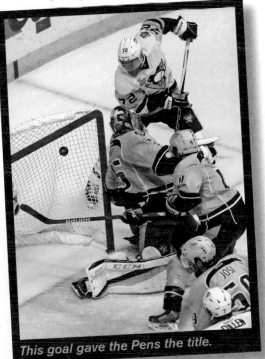

This goal gave the Pens the title.

Hockey Highlights

100th Anniversary?

The NHL celebrated its 100th anniversary in 2017—even though four of the Original Six teams are *not* 100 years old. How can that be? The league began play in 1917, but only two of today's teams existed back then: the Montreal Canadiens and the Toronto Maple Leafs. The Original Six teams were not actually the first six teams in the league. They're the six that survived after the Brooklyn Americans folded in 1942. The Canadiens, Maple Leafs, Chicago Blackhawks, Detroit Red Wings, Boston Bruins, and New York Rangers were the only teams in the league from 1942 to 1967.

Captain Connor

The Edmonton Oilers made headlines by making **Connor McDavid** the youngest captain in NHL history, at the age of 19 years and 266 days. Some people said McDavid was too young to lead his team. McDavid responded to the critics by scoring 100 points, winning both the Art Ross and Hart trophies, and leading the Oilers to their first playoff berth since 2006.

Streaking Blue Jackets

A season after they finished second to last in the East and hired **John Tortorella** as head coach, the Columbus Blue Jackets nearly made history in January. On November 29, 2016, the Jackets defeated the Tampa Bay Lightning 5–1—and they did not lose another game until January 5, 2017. The stretch included a perfect 14–0 December. A 5–0 loss to the Washington Capitals ended the Jackets' winning streak at 16 games—just one win short of the NHL record! Overall, Tortorella led Columbus to the best season in its franchise history, with 50 wins and 108 points. He was awarded the Jack Adams Trophy as best head coach.

He Keeps Going and Going

The elder statesman of the NHL, Florida Panthers forward **Jaromír Jágr**, continued to rewrite the record books this season. On December 22, 2016, Jágr scored his 1,888th point, passing **Mark Messier** for second place all-time in NHL scoring. Later in

Connor McDavid wore the captain's "C."

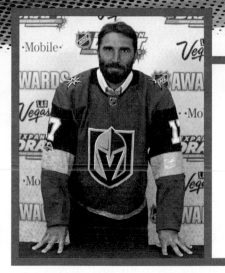

The Golden Knights

The NHL's newest team, the Vegas Golden Knights, began play in the 2017–18 season. (**Chris Thorburn** models their uniform at left.) The league held a special draft on June 21, allowing the Knights to take one player from each existing team. The Knights picked a team of young players, except for Nashville Predators forward **James Neal** and longtime Pittsburgh Penguins goaltender **Marc-Andre Fleury**.

the season, on the night he turned 45, Jágr celebrated by scoring his 1,900th career point!

A Dramatic Farewell

Carolina Hurricanes forward **Bryan Bickell**, who won three Stanley Cups with the Chicago Blackhawks, was diagnosed with multiple sclerosis in November 2016. After months of rehab, he rejoined his team in February 2017. But in April, Bickell made the difficult decision to retire at the end of the season. The team's very last game ended in a shootout, and Bickell made a goal on his final shot in the league.

O Canada!

Hockey was invented in Canada, but in the 2015–16 season, for the first time in 46 years, no Canadian teams made it to the playoffs. Fortunately for Canada, the 2016–17 season was a different story. Five of the seven Canadian teams qualified. Only the Vancouver Canucks and Winnipeg Jets missed. Even though Pittsburgh won the Cup, things are looking good for Canada!

The Hurricanes surround Bickell after his dramatic final goal.

2016 World Cup

Some of the best hockey was played before the NHL season even began. In September 2016, national teams from Canada, the Czech Republic, Finland, Russia, Sweden, and the United States—plus an all-star team from the rest of Europe and one from North America—put their best players on the ice for the World Cup of Hockey. Team North America was made up of players under 23 years old from Canada and the United States. **Auston Matthews**, **Connor McDavid**, **Johnny Gaudreau**, and others showed how bright the future of the game is. Of course, there was plenty of great veteran talent, too, including **Jonathan Toews**, **Sidney Crosby**, **Alex Ovechkin**, **Patrick Kane**, **Henrik Lundqvist**, and many other superstars.

The tournament had some shocking surprises and lots of exciting play. The US team, one of the favorites to win the gold medal, did not win a single game. Team North America's young stars battled hard but were knocked out of the tournament by a more experienced Russian team. As expected, Team Canada rolled over its opponents and earned a spot in the gold medal round against Team Europe. Europe boasted such stars as **Anze Kopitar** and **Zdeno Chára**. In the final, though, Team Canada used sensational goaltending from **Carey Price** and big goals in the final three minutes from **Brad Marchand** and **Patrice Bergeron** to take home the gold 2–1.

Team Canada's Carey Price, in action against Team Europe, was lights out in goal.

Women's World Championship

We're No. 1 . . . again! The US women won the Worlds.

American women have defeated Canada for the world title, and they have now won seven of the past eight World Championships.

The Americans almost skipped the 2017 event, though. In March, the women's team announced it would boycott (refuse to play) the event. The team believed the women's program was not treated fairly, even though the women's team was more successful! The players said that USA Hockey paid them far less than the men's team while still expecting them to train year-round for tournaments.

An overtime goal by **Hilary Knight** gave the United States Women's National Team a 3–2 victory over archrival Canada in the final game of the IIHF World Championships in April 2017.

It was the fourth time in a row that the

The women's team got support from the NHL and other pro male players. The men's team even threatened to boycott its own tournament! Three days before the World Championships, USA Hockey agreed to pay female players more and support women's hockey programs.

JUNIOR MEN WIN, TOO!

Team USA was also the big winner at the men's 2017 IIHF World Junior Championships. The American team didn't lose a game, going 7–0 and defeating Team Canada 5–4 in a shootout in the gold medal game. **Troy Terry** was the hero. He scored the only shootout goal, giving the USA its fourth gold medal in this event.

Olympics Letdown

To the disappointment of many fans, the NHL announced that it will not send players to the 2018 Winter Olympics in South Korea. It will be the first time that the NHL has not participated in the Olympics since 1994. NHL owners are against sending their players. They worry about injuries and losing money when the NHL takes an Olympics break.

2016-17 Awards

Hart Trophy
(Most Valuable Player)
Ted Lindsay Award
(MVP as voted by the players)
Art Ross Trophy
(Highest Scorer)
CONNOR McDAVID, Oilers

Vezina Trophy
(Best Goaltender)
SERGEI BOBROVSKY, Blue Jackets

Calder Trophy
(Best Rookie)
AUSTON MATTHEWS, Maple Leafs

Norris Trophy
(Best Defenseman)
BRENT BURNS, Sharks

Selke Trophy
(Best Defensive Forward)
PATRICE BERGERON, Bruins

Maurice Richard Trophy
(Top Goal Scorer)
SIDNEY CROSBY, Penguins

Lady Byng Trophy
(Sportsmanship)
JOHNNY GAUDREAU, Flames

Masterton Trophy
(Dedication to Hockey)
CRAIG ANDERSON, Senators

Jack Adams Award
(Coach of the Year)
JOHN TORTORELLA, Blue Jackets

Mark Messier Leadership Award
NICK FOLIGNO, Blue Jackets

Burns—and his award-worthy beard—won the Norris Trophy.

NHL Stat Leaders

100 POINTS
70 ASSISTS
Connor McDavid, Oilers

"He's one of the best skaters I've ever seen. He's able to do things at a high rate of speed, too, so he doesn't have to slow down in order to pass or shoot."

— ANAHEIM'S **RYAN GETZLAF** ON THE SKILLS OF SCORING LEADER CONNOR McDAVID

765

That is the career goals total of the remarkable **Jaromír Jágr**. The veteran center moved into third place all-time in 2017, trailing only **Wayne Gretzky** (894) and **Gordie Howe** (801) on the career goals list.

44 GOALS
Sidney Crosby, Penguins

34 PLUS-MINUS
Ryan Suter, Wild
Jason Zucker, Wild

2.06 GOALS AGAINST AVG.
.931 SAVE PERCENTAGE
Sergei Bobrovsky, Blue Jackets

42 GOALIE WINS
Braden Holtby, Capitals ▶▶▶
Cam Talbot, Oilers

Stanley Cup Champions

2016–17	**Pittsburgh Penguins**		1990–91	**Pittsburgh Penguins**
2015–16	**Pittsburgh Penguins**		1989–90	**Edmonton Oilers**
2014–15	**Chicago Blackhawks**		1988–89	**Calgary Flames**
2013–14	**Los Angeles Kings**		1987–88	**Edmonton Oilers**
2012–13	**Chicago Blackhawks**		1986–87	**Edmonton Oilers**
2011–12	**Los Angeles Kings**		1985–86	**Montreal Canadiens**
2010–11	**Boston Bruins**		1984–85	**Edmonton Oilers**
2009–10	**Chicago Blackhawks**		1983–84	**Edmonton Oilers**
2008–09	**Pittsburgh Penguins**		1982–83	**New York Islanders**
2007–08	**Detroit Red Wings**		1981–82	**New York Islanders**
2006–07	**Anaheim Ducks**		1980–81	**New York Islanders**
2005–06	**Carolina Hurricanes**		1979–80	**New York Islanders**
2004–05	No champion (Lockout)		1978–79	**Montreal Canadiens**
2003–04	**Tampa Bay Lightning**		1977–78	**Montreal Canadiens**
2002–03	**New Jersey Devils**		1976–77	**Montreal Canadiens**
2001–02	**Detroit Red Wings**		1975–76	**Montreal Canadiens**
2000–01	**Colorado Avalanche**		1974–75	**Philadelphia Flyers**
1999–00	**New Jersey Devils**		1973–74	**Philadelphia Flyers**
1998–99	**Dallas Stars**		1972–73	**Montreal Canadiens**
1997–98	**Detroit Red Wings**		1971–72	**Boston Bruins**
1996–97	**Detroit Red Wings**		1970–71	**Montreal Canadiens**
1995–96	**Colorado Avalanche**		1969–70	**Boston Bruins**
1994–95	**New Jersey Devils**		1968–69	**Montreal Canadiens**
1993–94	**New York Rangers**		1967–68	**Montreal Canadiens**
1992–93	**Montreal Canadiens**		1966–67	**Toronto Maple Leafs**
1991–92	**Pittsburgh Penguins**		1965–66	**Montreal Canadiens**

1964–65	**Montreal Canadiens**
1963–64	**Toronto Maple Leafs**
1962–63	**Toronto Maple Leafs**
1961–62	**Toronto Maple Leafs**
1960–61	**Chicago Blackhawks**
1959–60	**Montreal Canadiens**
1958–59	**Montreal Canadiens**
1957–58	**Montreal Canadiens**
1956–57	**Montreal Canadiens**
1955–56	**Montreal Canadiens**

MOST STANLEY CUP TITLES

Montreal Canadiens 23

Toronto Maple Leafs 13

Detroit Red Wings 11

Boston Bruins 6

Chicago Blackhawks 6

1954–55	**Detroit Red Wings**	1935–36	**Detroit Red Wings**
1953–54	**Detroit Red Wings**	1934–35	**Montreal Maroons**
1952–53	**Montreal Canadiens**	1933–34	**Chicago Blackhawks**
1951–52	**Detroit Red Wings**	1932–33	**New York Rangers**
1950–51	**Toronto Maple Leafs**	1931–32	**Toronto Maple Leafs**
1949–50	**Detroit Red Wings**	1930–31	**Montreal Canadiens**
1948–49	**Toronto Maple Leafs**	1929–30	**Montreal Canadiens**
1947–48	**Toronto Maple Leafs**	1928–29	**Boston Bruins**
1946–47	**Toronto Maple Leafs**	1927–28	**New York Rangers**
1945–46	**Montreal Canadiens**	1926–27	**Ottawa Senators**
1944–45	**Toronto Maple Leafs**	1925–26	**Montreal Maroons**
1943–44	**Montreal Canadiens**	1924–25	**Montreal Canadiens**
1942–43	**Detroit Red Wings**	1923–24	**Montreal Canadiens**
1941–42	**Toronto Maple Leafs**	1922–23	**Ottawa Senators**
1940–41	**Boston Bruins**	1921–22	**Toronto St. Patricks**
1939–40	**New York Rangers**	1920–21	**Ottawa Senators**
1938–39	**Boston Bruins**	1919–20	**Ottawa Senators**
1937–38	**Chicago Blackhawks**	1918–19	**Montreal Canadiens**
1936–37	**Detroit Red Wings**	1917–18	**Toronto Arenas**

SOCCER

RONALDO DOES IT AGAIN!
Though everyone on the pitch knows what he can do, somehow Cristiano Ronaldo still manages to get it done. In the 2017 Champions League final, he scored twice, including on this flick past the goalie as Real Madrid became repeat champs with a stirring 4–1 victory.

2016 MLS Recap

MLS Notes

→ Midfielder **Alphonso Davies** started a game for the Vancouver Whitecaps. Why is that news? Because he was just 15 years old! That made him the second youngest player in MLS history, behind 14-year-old **Freddy Adu** in 2004.

→ Was that **Landon Donovan** in a Galaxy uniform? Yes! Donovan retired in 2014 from a long career as one of the greatest American soccer players ever. But when his old team needed help late in the 2016 season, he pulled on his cleats and got back out there. He helped the Galaxy reach the 2016 conference semifinals.

→ MLS added two new teams in the 2017 season. Atlanta United and Minnesota United played their first games as the 21st and 22nd teams in the league–while MLS celebrated its 22nd birthday!

→ Top players from around the world have added great spice and skill to MLS. In 2017, two players stood out. The Galaxy added French striker **Romain Alessandrini**, and the Chicago Fire signed Serbian forward **Nemanja Nikolic**. Alessandrini became one of the highest-rated players in the league, winning several games for LA with late goals. Midway through the season, Nikolic took the league lead in goals scored!

Women's Pro Soccer

With just seconds left in overtime, it looked like the Western New York Flash would go home from the National Women's Soccer League championship disappointed. But a header by league MVP **Lynn Williams** (left) tied the score in the 124th minute. In the penalty-kick shootout to determine the champ, Flash goalie **Sabrina D'Angelo** made three brilliant saves of kicks by the Washington Spirit. Her final save clinched the first trophy for the Flash.

Game saver! Seattle's Stefan Frei made this amazing save to give his team a chance to win.

MLS 2016 Finals

Conference Championships: Heading into the Eastern Conference finals, Canadian fans knew that they'd have at least one team in MLS Cup 2017. Toronto FC faced the Montreal Impact for the Eastern crown. In the first of the two-game series, Montreal won at home 3–2. That set up the rematch in Toronto. Regular time ended with a 3–2 Toronto win. Since the winner was based on total goals, they had to play extra time. The hometown team poked in a pair of goals to make the two-game total 7–5. That sent Toronto to the championship game.

In the Western Conference finals, the goals were fewer but the action just as fierce. The Seattle Sounders beat the Colorado Rapids in both ends of the series. **Jordan Morris** scored in both games, including the only goal in the clincher.

MLS CUP 2016

One thing was for sure: There would be a new MLS champion in 2016. Both the Seattle Sounders and FC Toronto were going after their first title. The teams must have enjoyed the experience because they played through extra time without scoring.

A big reason for that was Seattle goalie **Stefan Frei**, who made several remarkable saves. The biggest came when he turned away a great header by Toronto's **Jozy Altidore**. Toronto players were already celebrating when Frei flew through the air.

The result sent the title chase to penalty kicks. Seattle's **Roman Torres** banged his in during sudden death to give the Sounders their first MLS championship. Seattle's fans have always been loyal supporters of their team, so the Sounders were happy to reward them with the trophy.

2017 Champions League

Mandzukic made a spectacular goal.

In the UEFA Champions League, Real Madrid returned to the title game for a record 12th time and for the second year in a row. Its opponent, Juventus, was also back on familiar ground. The famous Italian club was playing in its ninth Champions League final. But it had only won twice before, the last time in 1996.

Cristiano Ronaldo scored first for Madrid, but then **Mario Mandzukic** tied it for Juventus. He scored on a spectacular bicycle kick! But Madrid was too much. First, **Carlos Casemiro** blasted in a long shot to take the lead. Then Ronaldo touched in a perfect cross to make it 3–1. A late goal by **Marco Asensio** made the final score 4–1.

Real Madrid became the first team since 1990–and only the second ever–to repeat as Champions League winners. Ronaldo also became the first player to score in three Champions League finals.

RONALDO!

The debate about who is the best player in the world centers on two players— **Lionel Messi** and **Cristiano Ronaldo**. As great as Messi is, Ronaldo has been the hottest player lately. He led Portugal to the European Championship in 2016 and carried Real Madrid to its second straight Champions League title (right). In the final of that event, he scored his 600th career goal. His skills from long range and his creative play make him the most dangerous striker in soccer.

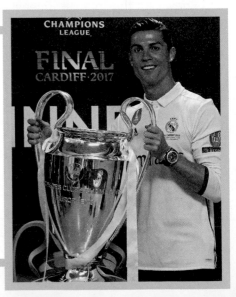

International Leagues
KEY 2017 CHAMPIONSHIPS

Barclay's Premier League (England)

The Chelsea Blues returned to the top for 2017. The London-based club started strong. Then it set a club record with 13 consecutive wins. After that, the Blues held off all challengers, including Tottenham United and Liverpool. It was their fifth title in the 2000s.

La Liga (Spain)

With **Lionel Messi**, **Neymar Jr.**, and **Luis Suárez** all available to score goals for you, your club is in great shape! That's what FC Barcelona enjoyed in the 2016–17 season, and that trio made the most of its chances. Together, the three international stars scored 79 of the team's 116 goals. However, it was not enough, and Real Madrid won its record 33rd La Liga championship.

Lionel Messi

Bundesliga (Germany)

Another year, another title—the fifth in a row—for the über-powerful Bayern Munich team. Its power starts at the back with captain and superstar goalie **Manuel Neuer**. Add in defensive strength from **Jerome Boateng** and **Marco Friedl** and scoring punch courtesy of **Robert Lewandowski** and **Arjen Robben**, and you've got a German superteam.

Ligue 1 (France)

Surprising AS Monaco won for the first time since 2000. A new coach, **Leonardo Jardim**, focused on young, fast, skilled players. The team ran away with the title.

Serie A (Italy)

Italy has seen some great soccer dynasties over the years, but in 2017, Juventus topped them all. The team that plays its home games in Turin won its sixth title in a row, setting a new record for consecutive Italian championships.

2018 World Cup Preview

The world's biggest sporting event (sorry, Olympics!) is coming in the summer of 2018. Billions of people around the world will be eagerly gobbling up the scores from the FIFA World Cup! The international soccer championship pits 32 national teams in an event to determine the world's best.

Countries played a long series of matches to qualify for the final round in Russia. Once they arrive, they'll play three games in their groups (see opposite page). The top two teams in each

SCHEDULE

World Cup Draw
Friday, December 1, 2017

Opening Game:
Thursday, June 14, 2018
10 AM Eastern time

Championship Game
Sunday, July 15, 2018
10 AM Eastern time

group will advance to the "knockout" stage. From then on, it's one loss and they're out!

Germany is the defending champion. It will be a team to watch. Brazil has won five World Cups, more than any other nation, and it will be aiming for a sixth. Argentina should have a shot, thanks to the great **Lionel Messi**. France looks strong, as does Chile, which has posted some big wins lately.

The United States won't know until October if it has made the finals. If the Americans do get in, it would extend their streak to eight World Cup trips in a row. The Americans have never gotten past the quarterfinals, but some young talent such as **Christian Pulisic** might help them go farther.

All the matches will be on live TV in the United States, so check your local listings and tune in next summer to the greatest (soccer) show on earth!

Germany won its fourth World Cup in 2014.

THE WORLD CUP TEAMS!

On December 1, a draw will create the eight groups of four teams that will play in the World Cup. After that happens, fill in the teams on the lines below and then cheer for your favorites!

GROUP A

GROUP B

GROUP C

GROUP D

GROUP E

GROUP F

GROUP G

GROUP H

Stat Stuff

MAJOR LEAGUE SOCCER
CHAMPIONS

2016	Seattle Sounders
2015	Portland Timbers
2014	Los Angeles Galaxy
2013	Sporting Kansas City
2012	Los Angeles Galaxy
2011	Los Angeles Galaxy
2010	Colorado Rapids
2009	Real Salt Lake
2008	Columbus Crew
2007	Houston Dynamo
2006	Houston Dynamo
2005	Los Angeles Galaxy
2004	D.C. United
2003	San Jose Earthquakes
2002	Los Angeles Galaxy
2001	San Jose Earthquakes
2000	Kansas City Wizards
1999	D.C. United
1998	Chicago Fire
1997	D.C. United
1996	D.C. United

UEFA CHAMPIONS
LEAGUE

The Champions League pits the best against the best. The top club teams from the members of UEFA (the Union of European Football Associations) face off in a months-long tournament.

2017	Real Madrid	SPAIN
2016	Real Madrid	SPAIN
2015	FC Barcelona	SPAIN
2014	Real Madrid	SPAIN
2013	Bayern Munich	GERMANY
2012	Chelsea FC	ENGLAND
2011	FC Barcelona	SPAIN
2010	Inter (Milan)	ITALY
2009	FC Barcelona	SPAIN
2008	Manchester United	ENGLAND
2007	AC Milan	ITALY
2006	FC Barcelona	SPAIN
2005	Liverpool FC	ENGLAND
2004	FC Porto	PORTUGAL
2003	AC Milan	ITALY
2002	Real Madrid	SPAIN
2001	Bayern Munich	GERMANY

WORLD CUP WINNERS

YEAR	CHAMPION	LOCATION
2018	_____	Russia
2014	**Germany**	Brazil
2010	**Spain**	South Africa
2006	**Italy**	Germany
2002	**Brazil**	South Korea/Japan
1998	**France**	France
1994	**Brazil**	United States
1990	**West Germany**	Italy
1986	**Argentina**	Mexico
1982	**Italy**	Spain
1978	**Argentina**	Argentina
1974	**West Germany**	West Germany
1970	**Brazil**	Mexico
1966	**England**	England
1962	**Brazil**	Chile
1958	**Brazil**	Sweden
1954	**West Germany**	Switzerland
1950	**Uruguay**	Brazil
1938	**Italy**	France
1934	**Italy**	Italy
1930	**Uruguay**	Uruguay

JJ WINS AGAIN!

Jimmie Johnson matched the great Richard Petty and Dale Earnhardt Sr. by winning his seventh NASCAR championship. He took advantage of a late crash in the final race to zoom to the title. For more on Johnson's title run and other NASCAR highlights, start your engines and turn the page!

A Season of Action!

The car says Earnhardt Jr., but the driver was really the recently "retired" Jeff Gordon.

The long NASCAR Sprint Cup season included 36 races, thousands of miles, gallons of fuel, acres of tires, and dozens of hard-working (and tired!) drivers. After the smoke of the final burnout cleared, the winner drove out . . . and it was a familiar face!

The 2016 season started with the closest Daytona 500 finish ever. **Denny Hamlin** squeaked ahead of **Martin Truex Jr.** to win by 1/100th of a second! A month later, **Kevin Harvick** matched that razor-thin margin when he beat **Carl Edwards** to the finish line in Phoenix. Fans and drivers alike loved the hard-charging, last-lap action and photo-finish results (unless you finished second!).

One of NASCAR's most popular drivers had to sit out much of the season. **Dale Earnhardt Jr.** suffered a concussion in a wreck at Michigan. While he healed, his team brought in another popular driver as a temporary replacement. The great **Jeff Gordon**, who had "retired" in 2015, jumped back into the driver's seat! Gordon didn't win, but he thrilled his fans with a few top-10 finishes.

Not all the action was in the Sprint Cup series. At a Camping World Truck Series race in September, the drama spilled off the track. On the final lap at the race in Canada, **John Hunter Nemechek** and **Cole Custer** banged doors over and over. The two ended the race skidding through the infield grass! NASCAR finally decided that Nemechek was the winner. While they waited for that result, Custer tackled Nemechek as he tried to grab the checkered flag!

Back on the Sprint Cup trail, in the race at Richmond that would determine the final Chase drivers, **Ryan Newman** felt like he

CHASE FOR THE CUP!

2016 FINAL STANDINGS

1. Jimmie **JOHNSON**
2. Joey **LOGANO**
3. Kyle **BUSCH**
4. Carl **EDWARDS**
5. Denny **HAMLIN**
6. Matt **KENSETH**
7. Kevin **HARVICK**
8. Kurt **BUSCH**
9. Austin **DILLON**
10. Martin **TRUEX JR.**
11. Chase **ELLIOTT**
12. Brad **KESELOWSKI**
13. Tony **STEWART**
14. Kyle **LARSON**
15. Jamie **McMURRAY**
16. Chris **BUESCHER**

got cheated. He had only a slim chance to make the Chase, but he wrecked. He blamed Tony Stewart for the wreck. Guess it was not just truck racers who had tempers!

Rookie driver Chase Elliott made the final Chase group. He earned a chance to match his dad, "Million Dollar" Bill, as a NASCAR champ. Other young stars such as Austin Dillon and Chris Buescher also made the Chase. Buescher can count his lucky stars for his spot. He won his first NASCAR race at Pocono in August when the race ended early due to rain. That was enough to help him squeak into his first Chase playoff.

Those young drivers would face off against some of the biggest names in the sport, including Jimmie Johnson, Carl Edwards, Kyle and Kurt Busch, and 2014 champ Harvick.

In the final race at Miami, with the Chase down to the final four drivers, Johnson used the skills that had made him one of the all-time greats and took the season-ending Victory Lap that every driver dreams of. JJ certainly knew the way!

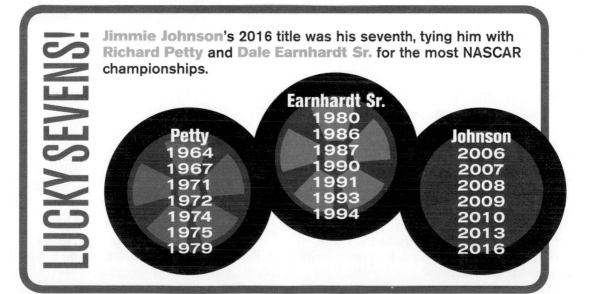

LUCKY SEVENS!

Jimmie Johnson's 2016 title was his seventh, tying him with Richard Petty and Dale Earnhardt Sr. for the most NASCAR championships.

Petty
1964
1967
1971
1972
1974
1975
1979

Earnhardt Sr.
1980
1986
1987
1990
1991
1993
1994

Johnson
2006
2007
2008
2009
2010
2013
2016

The Chase

The Chase for the Cup pits the top 16 racers in a 10-race playoff. During the season-ending Chase, the bottom drivers are dropped after every three races. In the end, the final four remaining racers battle in Miami to see who emerges as the season champion.

Challenger Round

CHICAGO: Martin Truex Jr. captured the first race of the 2016 Chase. He had to overcome a shredded tire and a late challenge from rookie Chase Elliott.

NEW HAMPSHIRE: Kevin Harvick made a big move toward a second series championship by winning here to clinch a spot in the next round.

DOVER: Truex won for the second time in three races, putting him in a great position as the first round ended. This marked the end of the road for a two-time champion, retiring Tony Stewart.

OUT: Tony Stewart, Chris Buescher, Kyle Larson, Jamie McMurray

Contender Round

CHARLOTTE: Hurricane Matthew drenched the track in North Carolina and set this race back a day. Jimmie Johnson zoomed through the pack to win for the first time since March. The six-time NASCAR champ earned a spot in the next round.

Logano was pumped by his Talladega win.

KANSAS: Harvick gave himself another chance at a NASCAR title by winning here with a sprint past Carl Edwards. The win put Harvick, the 2014 champ, into the next round.

TALLADEGA: Young driver Joey Logano, who won three Chase races in 2015, won here to clinch his spot in the final eight. He overcame driving out of pit row with a jack attached to his car! Denny Hamlin finished .006 seconds ahead of Kurt Busch. Why did that matter? That margin was enough for Hamlin to win a tiebreaker with Austin Dillon for the eighth and final spot in the next round!

OUT: Brad Keselowski, Martin Truex Jr., Austin Dillon, Chase Elliott

Eliminator Round

MARTINSVILLE: Six-time NASCAR champ Johnson clinched a spot in the Final Four with a win. Tire problems set back Edwards, who needed a win in one of the next two races.

TEXAS: Edwards came through! Though he was at the bottom in points, he was on top when this race was called due to rain. The surprising (and damp!) win put him into the Final Four in Miami.

PHOENIX: Logano punched his ticket for the Final Four with an "overtime" win at Phoenix. Late crashes forced several restarts. On the final one, Logano outran Kyle Busch to win the race. The finish gave him enough points to earn the final golden ticket. On to Miami for the big prize!

OUT: Matt Kenseth, Denny Hamlin, Kevin Harvick, Kurt Busch

Sprint Cup Championship

MIAMI: Edwards already had a pair of runner-up finishes in the season championship. For a while in this race, he thought he was in perfect position to win his first Sprint Cup. But with 10 laps to go, he and fellow Cup-chaser Logano collided. Edwards spun into the wall, and through the mess raced Johnson. Edwards ended up fourth among the Final Four. (In January 2017, Edwards announced that he was retiring from driving, ending a 13-year, 28-victory career.) Logano played follow-the-leader for miles, but he could not catch Johnson. Defending series champ Kyle Busch made some runs, too, but Johnson held them all off. As the checkered flag flew in the Florida evening, the veteran star won the race—and his seventh NASCAR title. That tied him with Dale Earnhardt Sr. and Richard Petty for the most season championships all-time.

Talk about confident! Johnson's team had his championship flag ready to fly in Miami.

Other NASCAR Champs

In his 14th season, Sauter won his first championship.

Camping World Truck Series

For the first time, NASCAR's truck series went to a Chase for the Cup playoff format. Sixteen drivers earned a spot. Johnny Sauter was one of them, having started the season off by winning at Daytona. He entered the Chase in fifth place and ended it in first. He did so thanks to victories in two of the Chase playoff races, at Martinsville and Texas. Sauter is a longtime driver who needed all of his experience to win. At one point in the final race, he was in 19th place. He inched his way back and passed former teammate Matt Crofton late to clinch the championship.

XFINITY SERIES

Drivers in NASCAR's No. 2 series don't usually make history. They are mostly just trying to win races and impress team owners in hopes of moving up to the top level. But in 2016, **Daniel Suárez** put his name in the motor racing history books. He clinched the season-long Xfinity Series championship when he won the season's final race at Miami. He became the first driver from Mexico to win any NASCAR title. Suarez grew up driving karts in Mexico. After moving to North Carolina to continue his racing career, he learned English partly by watching cartoons! After the race, he thanked fans in English and Spanish.

2016-17 NASCAR Highlights

Mr. Versatile ▶▶▶

Kyle Busch had raced at Martinsville in West Virginia 31 times before he finally finished in first place on his 32nd try. He won the 2016 Alpha Energy Solutions 250 on the famed short track. He had some practice there, since he won the Camping World Truck Series race the day before. Then, by winning the following Saturday at Texas in the XFinity and Sprint series, Busch accomplished a NASCAR first. He was the first driver to have four consecutive wins in three different machines!

Big Changes for 2017!

Goodbye, Sprint. Hello, Monster Energy! NASCAR changed its major sponsor for its top series. Monster Energy drink paid to have its name on the series championship chase. Also in 2017, NASCAR made changes to how races are scored. The winner still gets the most points, but other drivers have new chances to score. Each race is divided into three segments. The leaders of the first two segments each get 10 points; those following get points, too, based on where they are running. The winner of the race still takes home 40 points as well.

One for the Road

Tony Stewart showed that he still had what it takes to win. In the final season of his amazing career, he added one more trip to Victory Lane. He captured the checkered flag at Sonoma in April 2016—his first win in 84 starts. Though he exited the Chase early, it was a great way for this three-time champ to go out on top.

¡Bienvenidos, Daniel!

NASCAR fans south of the border have a new hero. **Daniel Suárez** became the first driver from Mexico to earn a ride at NASCAR's top level. He joined the Joe Gibbs team, steering the No. 19 car. He did pretty well, too, earning top-10 finishes in two of his first seven races as the 2017 season got off to a roaring start.

More Highlights

YOUNG WINNER!

Kaz Grala (No. 33 below) was just 18 when he won a Camping World Truck Series race at Daytona in February. He became the youngest driver to win any NASCAR race at the fabled Florida track. He managed to escape a second-lap wreck that knocked 17 cars out of the race and then another crash on the final lap. In that one, **Matt Crafton**'s truck was flipped end over end, but landed on its wheels! (No, he didn't keep driving it! And yes, he was fine!)

FIRST FOR BUSCH

Kurt Busch showed that what is behind you in NASCAR just might not matter. Thirty laps from the end of the 2017 Daytona 500, the rearview mirror fell off in his car. So he just kept his eyes on the road ahead! On the last lap, he passed several cars to earn his first win in NASCAR's most famous race.

32

That's how many times **Kurt Busch** took part in a NASCAR race at Daytona before finally finishing on top at the 2017 Daytona 500.

Goodbye, Junior

The most popular driver in NASCAR called it a career after the 2017 season. **Dale Earnhardt Jr.** wanted to go out on his own terms. He had missed much of 2016 with concussions. He got married in early 2017 and he and his wife decided that it would be wiser to hang up his helmet. "Junior" followed in the tracks of his father **Dale Sr.** as a popular star. Though Junior never did win a season title, he won 26 races (through mid-2017) and was in the top 10 about 40 percent of the time. Fans loved him. He was named Most Popular Driver 14 years in a row. Next up for Earnhardt fans: Dale Jr's nephew **Jeffrey** joined the racing family when he entered his first Daytona 500 in 2017.

ONE FOR GRANDPA!

Richard Childress is one of NASCAR's most successful car owners. His cars have been circling tracks since 1969. His cars and teams have won dozens of races and championships. But at the 2017 Coca-Cola 600, Childress added something very special to his list of accomplishments. He watched his grandson **Austin Dillon** (right) win NASCAR's longest race. It was Dillon's first NASCAR win, and it made Grandpa very proud indeed! Dillon is a former Truck Series and Xfinity Series champ, but he has struggled in the Cup series races. That is, until he outlasted the field in the 600!

NASCAR Champions

YEAR	DRIVER	CAR MAKER	YEAR	DRIVER	CAR MAKER
2016	Jimmie Johnson	Chevrolet	1995	Jeff Gordon	Chevrolet
2015	Kyle Busch	Toyota	1994	Dale Earnhardt Sr.	Chevrolet
2014	Kevin Harvick	Chevrolet	1993	Dale Earnhardt Sr.	Chevrolet
2013	Jimmie Johnson	Chevrolet	1992	Alan Kulwicki	Ford
2012	Brad Keselowski	Dodge	1991	Dale Earnhardt Sr.	Chevrolet
2011	Tony Stewart	Chevrolet	1990	Dale Earnhardt Sr.	Chevrolet
2010	Jimmie Johnson	Chevrolet	1989	Rusty Wallace	Pontiac
2009	Jimmie Johnson	Chevrolet	1988	Bill Elliott	Ford
2008	Jimmie Johnson	Chevrolet	1987	Dale Earnhardt Sr.	Chevrolet
2007	Jimmie Johnson	Chevrolet	1986	Dale Earnhardt Sr.	Chevrolet
2006	Jimmie Johnson	Chevrolet	1985	Darrell Waltrip	Chevrolet
2005	Tony Stewart	Chevrolet	1984	Terry Labonte	Chevrolet
2004	Kurt Busch	Ford	1983	Bobby Allison	Buick
2003	Matt Kenseth	Ford	1982	Darrell Waltrip	Buick
2002	Tony Stewart	Pontiac	1981	Darrell Waltrip	Buick
2001	Jeff Gordon	Chevrolet	1980	Dale Earnhardt Sr.	Chevrolet
2000	Bobby Labonte	Pontiac	1979	Richard Petty	Chevrolet
1999	Dale Jarrett	Ford	1978	Cale Yarborough	Oldsmobile
1998	Jeff Gordon	Chevrolet	1977	Cale Yarborough	Chevrolet
1997	Jeff Gordon	Chevrolet	1976	Cale Yarborough	Chevrolet
1996	Terry Labonte	Chevrolet	1975	Richard Petty	Dodge

YEAR	DRIVER	CAR MAKER	YEAR	DRIVER	CAR MAKER
1974	Richard Petty	Dodge	1961	Ned Jarrett	Chevrolet
1973	Benny Parsons	Chevrolet	1960	Rex White	Chevrolet
1972	Richard Petty	Plymouth	1959	Lee Petty	Plymouth
1971	Richard Petty	Plymouth	1958	Lee Petty	Oldsmobile
1970	Bobby Isaac	Dodge	1957	Buck Baker	Chevrolet
1969	David Pearson	Ford	1956	Buck Baker	Chrysler
1968	David Pearson	Ford	1955	Tim Flock	Chrysler
1967	Richard Petty	Plymouth	1954	Lee Petty	Chrysler
1966	David Pearson	Dodge	1953	Herb Thomas	Hudson
1965	Ned Jarrett	Ford	1952	Tim Flock	Hudson
1964	Richard Petty	Plymouth	1951	Herb Thomas	Hudson
1963	Joe Weatherly	Pontiac	1950	Bill Rexford	Oldsmobile
1962	Joe Weatherly	Pontiac	1949	Red Byron	Oldsmobile

2018 NASCAR HALL OF FAME CLASS

Red Byron: Though Byron had a short career as a driver, it was memorable. He won NASCAR's first race in 1948 along with the first two season championships in 1948 and 1949.

Ray Evernham: Evernham was the pit-road genius behind **Jeff Gordon's** famous "Rainbow Warriors" championship teams in 1995, 1997, and 1998. Together, the team made performing lightning-fast pit stops a part of every team's victory plan.

Roy Hornaday Jr.: Hornaday is the most successful driver ever in the Camping World Truck Series, with a record four season championships and 51 race victories.

Ken Squier: This broadcaster founded the Motor Racing Network and later called races for decades on national TV.

Robert Yates: The best engine builder in recent decades, Yates's machines powered NASCAR and Daytona 500 champs.

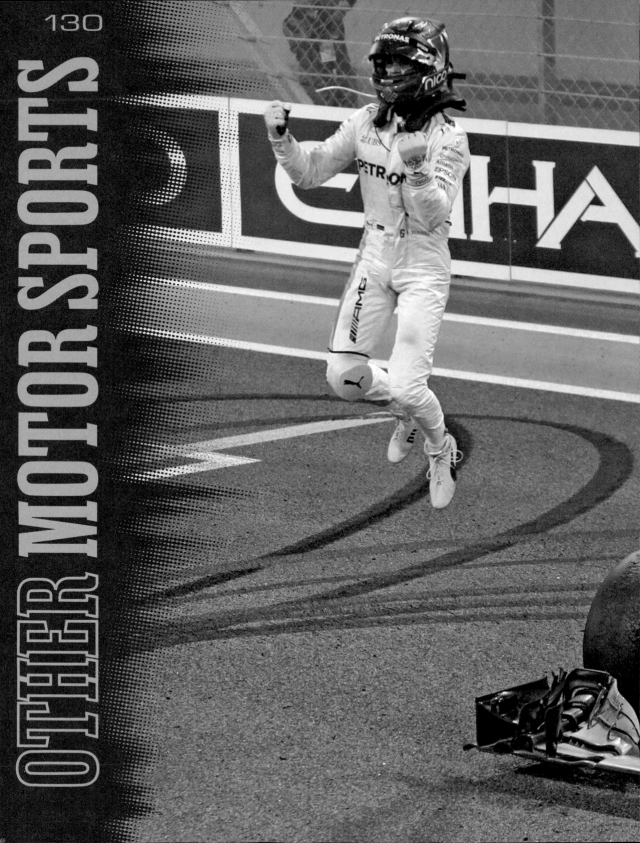

OTHER MOTORSPORTS

HELLO, CHAMP . . . AND GOODBYE!
Following in his champion father's tracks, Nico Rosberg won the Formula 1 drivers' championship. The German racer then surprised the sport by retiring after the season. Talk about going out in style . . . and on top!

2016 Formula 1

Germany's **Nico Rosberg** got off to a hot start in the 2016 Formula 1 season, winning the first three races. That gave him six victories in a row, since he won the final three races of 2015. Every driver who opened the season three-for-three went on to win the season title. Rosberg topped them by winning a fourth straight race in Russia.

However, British driving ace **Lewis Hamilton**, Rosberg's Mercedes teammate, knows a little bit about winning, too.

Hamilton has won three Formula 1 titles since 2008. He roared back into the season points lead by midway through the summer, coming from 43 points down to 19 points ahead.

Rosberg then won in Baku to move back into the lead. That race was the first ever held in the Central Asian nation of Azerbaijan. It was also one of a Formula 1-record 21 races in the season.

But then Hamilton won in Monaco,

This ancient castle provided a backdrop for Formula 1's first visit to Baku, Azerbaijan.

FUTURE STAR?

Driver **Max Verstappen** was a first . . . twice! By winning the Spanish Grand Prix, he became the first 18-year-old to win a race. He was the youngest Formula 1 winner ever by three years! He was also the first person from the Netherlands to win an F1 race. A crash by **Nico Rosberg** and **Lewis Hamilton** helped, but Verstappen took full advantage to pull ahead.

Canada, and Austria, followed by victories in Great Britain, Hungary, and Germany. Could Rosberg regain his early-season form?

He could. Rosberg won at Spa and Monza to inch close to Hamilton. Then in Malaysia, Hamilton blew an engine and lost crucial points. That gave Rosberg a lead he would never give up.

Like the champion he is, Hamilton never quit. He captured races in Texas, Mexico, and Brazil. But Rosberg continued to finish high in each race and maintain the points lead. In the final race of the season in Abu Dhabi, Hamilton again captured the checkered flag. But his late flurry of Ws was not enough to overcome Rosberg's season points total. Rosberg's second-place finish in Abu Dhabi put him five points ahead, making him a first-time Formula-1 champ.

He was not the first Rosberg to say that, however. In 1982, Nico's father, **Keke**, was also the world champion.

Not long after he won the title, the younger Rosberg shocked the sport by announcing his retirement. Who will pick up the crown in 2017?

2016 FORMULA 1 TOP DRIVERS

PLACE	DRIVER, TEAM	POINTS
1.	Nico **ROSBERG**, Mercedes	385
2.	Lewis **HAMILTON**, Mercedes	380
3.	Daniel **RICCIARDO**, Red Bull	256
4.	Sebastian **VETTEL**, Ferrari	212
5.	Max **VERSTAPPEN**, Red Bull	204

2016 IndyCar

French driver **Simon Pagenaud** won in only his second season with the Penske team, and his fifth season overall on the open-wheel circuit. He won three of the first five races of the season and held off a hard charge from former champ **Will Power** late in the summer.

The 2016 season included new races in Phoenix, Boston, and Road America in Wisconsin. Ratings had been going up for TV coverage, so fans got to see more action than ever.

There were many memorable events. **Josef Newgarden** impressed fellow drivers and fans alike by coming back just two weeks after a terrible practice accident to win in Iowa, even as he nursed a broken bone in his hand!

Fans enjoyed an amazing finish at the race in Texas. Rain moved the race day, and a rough track kept drivers bouncing around. In the end, a furious last lap ended when **Graham Rahal** passed **James Hinchcliffe**. Rahal nosed ahead to win

Simon Pagenaud guided his Indy car through the curves toward a fantastique finish!

2017 INDY 500
NEW CHAMP

The 101st running of this famous race featured an exciting finish and a scary crash. A last-lap duel between **Hélio Castroneves** of Brazil and **Takuma Sato** of Japan ended with Sato edging the three-time champ. It was the first Indy 500 win by a driver from Japan and only the second by Sato in 123 races. The veteran driver enjoyed the traditional milk shower in Victory Lane (left). Earlier in the race, **Scott Dixon**'s car went airborne after crashing into **Jay Howard**'s. Dixon's car flipped end over end, landing upside down at one point. Amazingly, both drivers walked away from the wreck without injury.

by .008 of a second. That's faster than the blink of an eye!

Perhaps the biggest challenger to Pagenaud all summer was Power of Australia. After missing some early races with a "concussion" (more on that in a moment), Power won four races in the summer to get close to the French driver. But a crash at Watkins Glen put him out of more races, and there was not enough time to catch up.

About that concussion: Doctors thought at first Power had suffered it in a practice session. Later, it was learned he just had an inner-ear infection. But IndyCar, like most sports, is taking concussions more seriously than ever. Even though the mistake caused him to miss races, Power was still in favor of the care taken. "You must be very careful when you are talking about the brain," he said.

In July, Pagenaud and Power dueled in the Mid-Ohio race. Pagenaud managed a key late pass for the victory. That was a springboard for him toward the end of the season. In 2016's final race, at Sonoma, only Power had a shot at catching Pagenaud. But the Frenchman roared away with the victory—his fifth of the year—to clinch the season title.

INDYCAR 2016
FINAL STANDINGS

DRIVER	POINTS
1. **Simon PAGENAUD**	659
2. **Will POWER**	532
3. **Helio CASTRONEVES**	504
4. **Josef NEWGARDEN**	502
5. **Graham RAHAL**	484
6. **Scott DIXON**	477
7. **Tony KANAAN**	461
8. **Juan Pablo MONTOYA**	433
Charlie KIMBALL	433
10. **Carlos MUÑOZ**	432

Drag Racing

Funny Car legend John Force must be the fastest-driving grandpa in America.

TOP FUEL

Former motorcycle racer **Antron Brown** has proved that he made the right choice by switching to the Top Fuel division. A few years ago, he moved from two wheels to four, and he has become a star. He won his third season title with the points he earned at the Las Vegas event in late October.

FUNNY CAR

John Force is proving that in racing, older can be better! He's 67 and can still outrace the kids. He won multiple events in the 2016 season. At the Las Vegas race, he beat his daughter Courtney in the final!

PRO STOCK

Like a drag race should, the battle for this one went down to the wire. **Jason Line** earned his third pro stock title on the final day of the season. His semifinal win at the NHRA Finals gave him enough points to nip **Greg Anderson**. Anderson then won the event at the Pomona track, but it was too late to catch Line.

PRO STOCK MOTORCYCLE

Jerry Savoie became the only first-time champion of the 2016 season. It took losses by his two closest competitors to give Savoie the title. Savoie will take his trophy home to his offseason job—working at an alligator farm!

Motorcycle Racing

MotoGP

Marc Márquez (below) won the 2016 Japan Grand Prix—his fifth victory of the season—and clinched the championship with three races still to go in the season. It was the third world title for the young rider from Spain. Márquez had to battle defending champ **Jorge Lorenzo**, who started hot with three early race wins but faded over the summer. In all, eight different riders won at least one race—the most all-time for MotoGP. In its 68th season of high-speed motorcycle racing, it looks like there are more great riders than ever.

SUPERCROSS

In the 450cc class in the 2017 AMA Supercross series, **Eli Tomac** made it a battle all season long. He stayed right behind three-time defending champ **Ryan Dungey** to the final race at Las Vegas. Tomac needed to finish ahead of Dungey by nine points, but in the end could not climb that final hill. Dungey wrapped up his third straight Supercross championship with a fourth place finish. Showing how close the competition is getting in this rough-and-tumble sport, this was the first time that Dungey needed a result in the final event to clinch the title. In the 250cc class, **Zach Osborne** almost saw his championship chances disappear after a first-lap crash in Las Vegas. But he stormed back to finish with the points he needed to win his first national championship.

MOTOCROSS

Eli Tomac made up for his near-miss in Supercross by finishing on top of the 2017 Lucas Oil Motocross 450 Class outdoor championship. Tomac became the 11th rider to be national champ in the 250 and 450 classes. He won the 250 in 2013. Tomac almost blew it in the first moto in the final event in Buffalo. He fell early in the race, but got back up with enough time to finish fifth. That helped him get the points he needed to win it all. Zach Osborne won the 250 Class this year; now he can shoot for the "double" like Tomac!

Major Champions
OF THE 2000s

TOP FUEL DRAGSTERS

YEAR	DRIVER
2016	Antron Brown
2015	Antron Brown
2014	Tony Schumacher
2013	Shawn Langdon
2012	Antron Brown
2011	Del Worsham
2010	Larry Dixon
2009	Tony Schumacher
2008	Tony Schumacher
2007	Tony Schumacher
2006	Tony Schumacher
2005	Tony Schumacher
2004	Tony Schumacher
2003	Larry Dixon
2002	Larry Dixon
2001	Kenny Bernstein

FUNNY CARS

YEAR	DRIVER
2016	Ron Capps
2015	Del Worsham
2014	Matt Hagan
2013	John Force
2012	Jack Beckman
2011	Matt Hagan
2010	John Force
2009	Robert Hight
2008	Cruz Pedregon
2007	Tony Pedregon
2006	John Force
2005	Gary Scelzi
2004	John Force
2003	Tony Pedregon
2002	John Force
2001	John Force

PRO STOCK CARS

YEAR	DRIVER
2016	Jason Line
2015	Erica Enders-Stevens
2014	Erica Enders-Stevens
2013	Jeg Coughlin Jr.
2012	Allen Johnson
2011	Jason Line
2010	Greg Anderson
2009	Mike Edwards
2008	Jeg Coughlin Jr.
2007	Jeg Coughlin Jr.
2006	Jason Line
2005	Greg Anderson
2004	Greg Anderson
2003	Greg Anderson
2002	Jeg Coughlin Jr.
2001	Warren Johnson

FORMULA 1

YEAR	DRIVER
2016	Nico Rosberg
2015	Lewis Hamilton
2014	Lewis Hamilton
2013	Sebastian Vettel
2012	Sebastian Vettel
2011	Sebastian Vettel
2010	Sebastian Vettel
2009	Jenson Button
2008	Lewis Hamilton
2007	Kimi Räikkönen
2006	Fernando Alonso
2005	Fernando Alonso
2004	Michael Schumacher
2003	Michael Schumacher
2002	Michael Schumacher
2001	Michael Schumacher

INDYCAR SERIES

YEAR	DRIVER
2016	Simon Pagenaud
2015	Scott Dixon
2014	Will Power
2013	Scott Dixon
2012	Ryan Hunter-Reay
2011	Dario Franchitti
2010	Dario Franchitti
2009	Dario Franchitti
2008	Scott Dixon
2007	Dario Franchitti
2006	Sam Hornish Jr.
2005	Dan Wheldon
2004	Tony Kanaan
2003	Scott Dixon
2002	Sam Hornish Jr.
2001	Sam Hornish Jr.

AMA SUPERCROSS

YEAR	DRIVER
2017	Ryan Dungey
2016	Ryan Dungey
2015	Ryan Dungey
2014	Ryan Villopoto
2013	Ryan Villopoto
2012	Ryan Villopoto
2011	Ryan Villopoto
2010	Ryan Dungey
2009	James Stewart Jr.
2008	Chad Reed
2007	James Stewart Jr.
2006	Ricky Carmichael
2005	Ricky Carmichael
2004	Chad Reed
2003	Ricky Carmichael
2002	Ricky Carmichael
2001	Ricky Carmichael

AMA MOTOCROSS

YEAR	RIDER (MOTOCROSS)	RIDER (LITES)
2017	TK	
2016	Ken Roczen	Cooper Webb
2015	Ryan Dungey	Jeremy Martin
2014	Ken Roczen	Jeremy Martin
2013	Ryan Villopoto	Eli Tomac
2012	Ryan Dungey	Blake Baggett
2011	Ryan Villopoto	Dean Wilson
2010	Ryan Dungey	Trey Canard
2009	Chad Reed	Ryan Dungey
2008	James Stewart Jr.	Ryan Villopoto
2007	Grant Langston	Ryan Villopoto
2006	Ricky Carmichael	Ryan Villopoto
2005	Ricky Carmichael	Ivan Tedesco
2004	Ricky Carmichael	James Stewart Jr.
2003	Ricky Carmichael	Grant Langston
2002	Ricky Carmichael	James Stewart Jr.
2001	Ricky Carmichael	Mike Brown

RUBBERBAND MAN
Levi Sherwood bent over backwards to win the gold medal in Moto X Freestyle at the Summer X Games in Minneapolis in 2017. The New Zealander also took first place in the Moto X Best Trick competition.

Summer X Games

The Summer X Games moved to the Midwest for the first time in 2017. US Bank Stadium in Minneapolis, Minn., kicked off a big year—it would also serve as the site of Super Bowl LII in February 2018—by hosting some of the world's most amazing athletes.

Zach Newman competes in the BMX Vert final.

Lucky 13th

Brighton Zeuner narrowly missed a medal at her X Games debut in 2016, when she finished fourth in Skateboard Park. With that experience behind her, the grizzled veteran returned to the X Games in 2017 to set her sights on gold . . . and she was only 12! Actually, Zeuner turned 13 the day before the Skate Park final in 2017. But she put her celebration on hold until after wowing the crowd with a winning run that made her the youngest gold medalist in X Games history. "This is the best birthday in my entire life!" she said. "I can't wait to go celebrate!"

Big Air Is Back!

There were no winds to worry about inside in Minneapolis like there were outside in Austin, Texas, in 2016. That year, 30-mile-per-hour winds made it too dangerous for skateboards and bikes—and their riders!—to scale the 82-foot-high MegaRamp. So a couple of the most popular X Games competitions were canceled. They returned in 2017, however, since the US Bank Stadium had plenty of room to fit the ramp. **James Foster** won the BMX Big Air competition, and **Eliot Sloan** took home the gold in Skateboard Big Air.

Hometown Star

Alec Majerus was right at home while winning a silver medal in the Skateboard Street competition. Really. A native of Rochester, Minn., Majerus often made the 90-minute drive to Minneapolis to skate the downtown streets there. He sent the X Games crowd into a frenzy with a backside flip over the Viking ship in the center of the

2017 SUMMER X GAMES CHAMPS

BMX BIG AIR	**James Foster**	MOTO X QUARTERPIPE	**Colby Raha**
BMX DIRT	**Colton Walker**	MOTO X STEP UP	**Jarryd McNeil**
BMX PARK	**Kevin Peraza**	SKATEBOARD BIG AIR	**Elliot Sloan**
BMX PARK BEST TRICK	**Kyle Baldock**	M SKATEBOARD PARK	**Alex Sorgente**
BMX STREET	**Garrett Reynolds**	W SKATEBOARD PARK	**Brighton Zeuner**
BMX VERT	**Vince Byron**	M SKATEBOARD STREET	**Kelvin Hoefler**
HARLEY-DAVIDSON FLAT TRACK	**Sammy Halbert**	W SKATEBOARD STREET	**Aori Nishimura**
MOTO X BEST TRICK	**Levi Sherwood**	SKATEBOARD ST. AMATEURS	**Jagger Eaton**
MOTO X BEST WHIP	**Destin Cantrell**	SKATEBOARD VERT	**Moto Shibata**
MOTO X FREESTYLE	**Levi Sherwood**		

"I couldn't be more stoked. . . .
I wanted to send it for Mirra, like he used to do it for us."
—AUSTRALIA'S **KYLE BALDOCK**, AFTER WINNING THE "GOLDEN PEDAL" AS THE WINNER OF THE DAVE MIRRA BMX BEST TRICK,
NAMED IN HONOR OF THE LATE INTERNATIONAL SUPERSTAR.

Skate Street course late in his final run. That helped him earn the silver medal. Brazil's **Kelvin Hoefler** won the gold.

Summer X Notes

* After more than two decades of competition and a record 30 X Games medals, legendary Big Air star **Bob Burnquist** hung up his board after the Games in Minneapolis. His tears at the end were not out of sadness, but out of gratitude for the many years of memories.

* **Aori Nishimura** became the first female Japanese athlete to win a gold medal in skateboarding at the X Games. The 15-year-old had a flawless first run in the Skateboard Street final that vaulted her into first place, and she never gave up the lead.

Nishimura made history.

Winter X Games

A series of winter storms dumped several feet of snow in the Aspen area in the month leading up to the Winter X Games of January 26–29, 2017. The athletes took to the fresh powder like, well, fish to water and turned in some memorable performances.

There was no shortage of snow at the Winter X Games in Aspen in 2017.

Teen Sweep

Kelly Sildaru is such a star in her native Estonia that home-country reporters made the 5,000-mile trek to cover her at the X Games in Aspen. The group wasn't disappointed, as the Slopestyle star—who didn't turn 15 years old until a few weeks after the Games—won the event for the second consecutive year. Sildaru was joined on the podium by a couple of other not-yet-20-somethings. Tess Ledeux, 15, of France won silver in her X Games debut, and **Johanne Killi**, 19, of Norway took the bronze.

Back to the Basics

American **Elena Hight** has made a name for herself in the Snowboard SuperPipe with some huge tricks. At the 2013 X Games in Aspen, for instance, she landed the first double backside alley-oop rodeo during a halfpipe competition. She settled for silver that year, however, and had not returned to the podium since. So in 2017, Hight decided to concentrate on the fundamentals and emphasize process over results. In the end, the strategy paid off: In her 13th X Games appearance, she won her first gold medal.

Winter Strikes Back

The X Games are all about some of the world's most incredible competitors taming the snow with their amazing athletic feats. But sometimes, the elements and the courses have their day. One such time came during the Ski SuperPipe, when zero-degree temperatures made for especially icy and fast conditions that made the competition treacherous. Of the 22 runs in the event, 18 resulted in falls, with every skier crashing at least once. In the end, the survivor—er, winner—was Colorado native **Aaron Blunck**.

Noteworthy

* Most X Games participants learned to ski and snowboard in snow-heavy areas of the United States such as Colorado or in frigid countries in Northern Europe. Not **James Woods**. The Ski Big Air champ was born and raised in Great Britain, where he learned his craft on the dry slopes of the snowless Sheffield Ski Village.

* Colorado native **Taylor Gold** was a silver medalist in the men's Snowboard SuperPipe. He is the older brother of **Arielle Gold**, who was a silver medalist in the women's Snowboard SuperPipe in Aspen in 2016. The two were teammates on the US Winter Olympics Team in 2014.

* For the first time, women competitors got a chance to show their stuff in Big Air competition in Aspen. Germany's **Lisa Zimmerman**, already the winner of several Big Air competitions previously around the world, won Ski Big Air. American **Hailey Langland** won the Snowboard Big Air.

* BikeCross—think supercross on snow—made its X Games debut in Aspen. The amazing snow bikes don't handle so much like a snowmobile as they do a motorcycle. Canada's **Brock Hoyer** handled his snow bike the best and won the gold medal.

2016 WINTER X GAMES CHAMPS

M SKI BIG AIR	**James Woods**	M SNOWBOARD BIG AIR	**Max Parrot**
W SKI BIG AIR	**Lisa Zimmermann**	W SNOWBOARD BIG AIR	**Hailey Langland**
M SKI SLOPESTYLE	**Øystein Braaten**	M SNOWBOARD SLOPESTYLE	**Marcus Kleveland**
W SKI SLOPESTYLE	**Kelly Sildaru**	W SNOWBOARD SLOPESTYLE	**Julia Marino**
M SKI SUPERPIPE	**Aaron Blunck**	M SNOWBOARD SUPERPIPE	**Scotty James**
W SKI SUPERPIPE	**Marie Martinod**	W SNOWBOARD SUPERPIPE	**Elena Hight**
SNOW BIKECROSS	**Brock Hoyer**	SNOWMOBILE FREESTYLE	**Joe Parsons**
SNOWMOBILE BEST TRICK	**Daniel Bodin**	SNOWMOBILE SNOCROSS	**Petter Narsa**
SNOWMOBILE SNOCROSS ADAPTIVE	**Mike Schultz**		

Action Notes

Crashed Ice ▶▶▶

Cameron Naasz of the United States and **Jacqueline Legere** of Canada were the men's and women's world champions for 2017 in Red Bull Crashed Ice. Crashed ice? That's right. One of the most extreme of extreme sports has held official competitions since the early 2000s. Crashed ice is a downhill race that is sort of a combination of skiing, ice hockey, and bobsledding. Racers often have a hockey background and wear uniforms and helmets similar to those in that sport. Such protection is needed on the steep turns, jumps, and high drops of a crashed-ice course. Naasz and Legere both are ice hockey veterans, and when Legere is not on the crashed-ice course, she is a professional stuntwoman.

Need for Speed, Part I

In the fall of 2016, Denver native **Kyle Wester** set out to break the world record for the fastest speed on a skateboard. (Warning: For experts only!) Before Wester's attempt, the fastest recorded mark was 81.2 miles per hour. Wester found a downhill stretch of road in Colorado, made sure it was totally clear of other traffic, and obliterated the mark by zipping along at 89.4 miles per hour.

Need for Speed, Part II

At the famed Bonneville Salt Flats in Utah, many land speed records have been set over the years. In January 2017, San Diego's **Denise Mueller** set the latest. She hopped on her customized bike and hitched a ride behind a pace car that pulled her along at 90 miles per hour. Then she unhooked from the car but kept drafting behind it, pedaling furiously but smoothly until she reached an amazing 147 miles per hour. It was a new women's bicycle record, and it gave Mueller another goal. She immediately set her sights on the all-time mark, by a man or woman, of 167 miles per hour, set in 1995 by Fred Rompleberg.

Surf's Up!

John John Florence grew up in a house just off the Bonzai Pipeline in Hawaii. The famed reef break creates huge waves that are a surfer's dream. Florence was surfing on his own by the time he was five and competing on the World Surf League tour at 16. In 2016, at age 24, he became the first Hawaiian in 12 years to win the men's tour championship. Then he picked up in 2017 right where he left off, finishing in the top three (with one victory) in the first three events of the season.

Tyler Wright also grew up in a surf spot, though far away from Hawaii, at Culberra Beach, Australia. The 22-year-old won four events in 2016 to take her first overall women's title, then threatened to run away with the 2017 crown by building a sizable lead at the season's halfway point.

Kitesurfer in Chief

Freed from the burdens of watching over the economy and keeping the world safe for democracy, former president **Barack Obama** enjoyed some action sports in 2017. In February, not long after leaving office, he took to kitesurfing in the British Virgin Islands. The president's form? Well, let's just say he was a bit rusty, and he spent a lot of time in the water. But that's okay. He'd been a little busy the previous eight years.

John John Florence—and a drone!—navigate the waves.

GOLF

**HATS OFF
TO THE CHAMP!**
*Jordan Spieth
acknowledges the
applause after closing
out his three-stroke
victory at the British
Open in the summer of
2017. It was the third
major-championship title
of the young American
star's career.*

Major Moments

Less than one week before his 24th birthday, American **Jordan Spieth** won the 2017 British Open for his third career victory in a major golf championship. Spieth had previously won the Masters and the US Open. His British Open win put him in some elite company: The only other player to win three legs of the majors before he turned 24 was the legendary **Jack Nicklaus**. (Nicklaus went on to win a record 18 major titles.)

At England's Royal Birkdale Golf Club, Spieth made three birdies and an eagle from the 14th through 17th holes to beat runner-up **Matt Kuchar** by three strokes. But it was an amazing bogey on the 13th hole that saved the tournament for him. Spieth and Kuchar came to that hole tied for the lead, but Spieth drove the ball so far out of play that he had to take a penalty stroke. His best chance for his next shot came from the driving range! After his penalty drop on the range, he hit the ball close enough to the green to chip on and make a clutch putt. Instead of being two or three shots behind, he was only one back. He erased that deficit with a birdie at the next hole, then dropped a 45-foot putt for eagle at the 15th to take control of the tournament.

Garcia finally mastered a major.

While Spieth had become used to winning majors at a young age, many golf fans wondered if **Sergio Garcia** would ever win one. The 37-year-old Spaniard long has been one of the best golfers in the world, winning tournaments all around the globe. But he entered 2017 with the dreaded unofficial title of Best Player Never to Win a Major. Sergio finally tossed that aside by winning the season's first major, the Masters, in April. Garcia edged England's **Justin Rose** with a birdie on the first extra hole after the two players finished Round 4 in a tie. Garcia's win came in his 74th career appearance in a major.

American **Brooks Koepka** also won his first major in 2017, but the 27-year-old's victory at the US Open in June came in just his 15th career major appearance. At 16-under, Koepka won by four strokes and equaled the lowest score in relation to par in US Open history.

The PGA Championship saw another first-time winner, **Justin Thomas**.

2017 MEN'S MAJORS

MASTERS	**Sergio Garcia**
US OPEN	**Brooks Koepka**
BRITISH OPEN	**Jordan Spieth**
PGA CHAMPIONSHIP	**Justin Thomas**

LPGA 2017

Kang's first trophy was a big one!

American **Danielle Kang** had never won an event—yet alone won a major—on the LPGA Tour before. So it might have looked as if the pressure was getting to her on the 10th hole of the final round of the Women's PGA Championship at Olympia Fields, Ill., in the summer of 2017. Kang, who was in contention to win, missed a very short putt and took a bogey. Instead of bowing to the pressure, though, the 24-year-old from San Francisco transformed the bad hole into a turning point. "I'm going to learn from that," she said to herself. She sure did! Kang, a two-time US Women's Amateur winner who played college golf at Pepperdine, birdied each of the next four holes. She added another birdie on the final hole and held off 19-year-old Canadian **Brooke Henderson** to win by one shot.

Two weeks later, another young LPGA star made her first career victory a major win. **Sung Hyun Park**, a 23-year-old rookie from South Korea, won the US Women's Open at Bedminster, N.J., by two shots over countrywoman **Hye Jin Choi**. Park made six birdies in the final round, including three without a bogey on the crucial back nine.

So Yeon Ryu, on the other hand, already had experience at winning when she entered the final round of the ANA Inspiration, the 2017 season's first major championship, just three shots out of the lead. The South Korean golfer had three career victories, including the 2011 US Women's Open. But she had not won on tour since 2014. She ended that drought with a flawless final round in which she birdied four holes and did not make a bogey. She carded another birdie on the first hole of a playoff with **Lexi Thompson** to win the tournament.

It was back to first-time winners at the Women's British Open when **In-Kyung Kim** captured the title in Scotland.

LPGA MAJOR WINNERS

ANA INSPIRATION	**So Yeon Ryu**
WOMEN'S PGA	**Danielle Kang**
US WOMEN'S OPEN	**Sung Hyun Park**
WOMEN'S BRITISH OPEN	**In-Kyung Kim**
EVIAN CHAMPIONSHIP	_____

Ryder Cup Report

Professional golfers are used to competing as individuals for prize money. But once every two years, golfers team up to represent squads from the United States and Europe in the sport's most prestigious competition: the Ryder Cup. There's no prize money on the line, just a considerable amount of national pride.

In 2016, the American Ryder Cup team was under a lot of pressure to restore its pride. US golfers had not won the international event since 2008 (and had lost eight of the previous 10 Cups). But at the Hazeltine National Golf Club in Chaska, Minn., the 12 US golfers responded with a convincing 17–11 victory over Europe to bring the Cup back to America. **Ryan Moore**, who was the last golfer added to the squad by captain **Davis Love III**, rolled in a birdie putt to win his match against **Lee Westwood** for the clinching points.

In the three-day event, golfers play several types of matches. On the first day, the United States stormed to a 4–0 lead but stumbled in the afternoon. After Day 2, the Americans led 9.5–6.5. They had lost other leads in the past, however, so Sunday's head-to-head singles matches were intense.

In front of a loud and (mostly) pro-United States crowd, Americans **Patrick Reed** and **Rickie Fowler** notched early wins on the final day. Reed beat 2016 FedEx Cup champ **Rory McIlroy**, while Fowler defeated Olympic gold medalist **Justin Rose**. Americans **Brooks Koepka** and **Brandt Snedeker** also won their matches. A clutch birdie putt on the final hole helped veteran **Phil Mickelson** tie **Sergio Garcia**, giving each side half a point. Together, those two stars combined for 19 birdies in their thrilling match.

When Moore beat Lee Westwood, the US team had enough points to win the Cup. Then **Zach Johnson** and **Dustin Johnson** also won their matches to give the Americans their final total of 17 points.

Captain Davis Love III (in the white shirt) and the Americans celebrated the victory.

Chip Shots

$10 Million Putt

Rory McIlroy made a 13-foot putt on the fourth hole of a sudden-death playoff to win the 2016 Tour Championship. That gave him enough points to also win the $10 million FedEx Cup. McIlroy had scrambled during the day to make it into the three-man playoff. Then he had three chances to win before finally nailing the birdie. It was the first FedEx Cup title for the great young star from Northern Ireland.

Rising Star

Justin Thomas was overshadowed early in his PGA career by **Jordan Spieth**, a fellow member of a great group of young golfers who graduated from high school in 2011. But in 2017, Thomas stepped out of the shadows. He began the calendar year by winning the

tournament for 2016 champions in Hawaii. The next week, he won again when he became the youngest player ever to shoot 59 on the PGA Tour. Thomas and Spieth have remained close friends from their days in youth golf. But now it's game on!

No Cash Reward

Finishing in second place at the US Women's Open in 2017 was worth a whopping $540,000 . . . except that it wasn't. Normally, the tournament runner-up would have received that much, but second place went to surprising amateur **Hye Jin Choi**. Because the South Korean was not a professional, she was not allowed to collect the prize money. Choi, who nearly became the first amateur in 50 years to win the US Women's Open, was only 17 at the time. There will probably be many more golf paychecks in her future.

Rory McIlroy

Experience Counts ▶▶▶

In 2016, 25 of the 33 events on the LPGA Tour were won by players 25 years or younger. The oldest winner was just 30! The trend continued in 2017. World No. 1 **Lydia Ko** turned only 20 in the spring. Tournament winners included 19-year-old **Brooke Henderson** and 22-year-old Lexi Thompson. But don't count out the 30-somethings (and 40-somethings!) just yet. Several months before her 40th birthday, **Cristie Kerr** posted a tournament-record score to win the Lotte Championship in Hawaii. "Experience is huge," she said after the win. "It's an advantage."

Marathon Man

You won't find **Barry Gibbons**'s name atop any PGA Tour leaderboard. But there's a good chance you might find him at your local municipal course.

That's because Barry plays a lot of golf—and we mean a lot! On December 31, the retired 57-year-old from Connecticut completed his 878th round of golf in 2016. That set an official Guinness World Record for the most rounds of golf in a year, walking. Gibbons covered 6,401 miles while carrying his bag, and he logged more than 12.7 million steps. "People are either envious," he says, "or they think I'm nuts."

442 That's how many major championships had been played in men's golf history before the British Open in the summer of 2017. In all those tournaments, no player ever shot a round better than 63. (American **Johnny Miller's** Sunday 63 to win the US Open at Oakmont in 1973 was the most famous of several such rounds.) South African golfer **Branden Grace** (left) finally broke the barrier in the third round at Royal Birkdale. Grace carded eight birdies and no bogeys. He made a short putt for par at the last hole to shoot 62. Despite that great round, Grace followed his big round on Saturday with a 70 on Sunday and finished tied for sixth in the tournament.

The Majors

In golf, some tournaments are known as the majors. They're the most important events of the year on the men's and women's pro tours. (There are four men's majors and five women's majors.) Among the men, **Jack Nicklaus** holds the record for the most all-time wins in the majors. **Patty Berg** won more majors than any other women's player.

MEN'S

	MASTERS	US OPEN	BRITISH OPEN	PGA CHAMP.	TOTAL
Jack **NICKLAUS**	6	4	3	5	**18**
Tiger **WOODS**	4	3	3	4	**14**
Walter **HAGEN**	0	2	4	5	**11**
Ben **HOGAN**	2	4	1	2	**9**
Gary **PLAYER**	3	1	3	2	**9**
Tom **WATSON**	2	1	5	0	**8**
Bobby **JONES**	0	4	3	0	**7**
Arnold **PALMER**	4	1	2	0	**7**
Gene **SARAZEN**	1	2	1	3	**7**
Sam **SNEAD**	3	0	1	3	**7**
Harry **VARDON**	0	1	6	0	**7**

RYDER CUP RESULTS

Note: The current format of the United States versus Europe began in 1979.

YEAR	WINNING TEAM	SCORE	YEAR	WINNING TEAM	SCORE
2016	**UNITED STATES**	17–11	1995	**EUROPE**	14.5–13.5
2014	**EUROPE**	16.5–11.5	1993	**UNITED STATES**	15–13
2012	**EUROPE**	14.5–13.5	1991	**UNITED STATES**	14.5–13.5
2010	**EUROPE**	14.5–13.5	1989	**TIE**	14–14
2008	**UNITED STATES**	16.5–11.5	1987	**EUROPE**	15–13
2006	**EUROPE**	18.5–9.5	1985	**EUROPE**	16.5–11.5
2004	**EUROPE**	18.5–9.5	1983	**UNITED STATES**	14.5–13.5
2002	**EUROPE**	15.5–12.5	1981	**UNITED STATES**	18.5–9.5
1999	**UNITED STATES**	14.5–13.5	1979	**UNITED STATES**	17–11
1997	**EUROPE**	14.5–13.5			

WOMEN'S

	LPGA	USO	BO	ANA	EV	MAUR	TH	WES	TOTAL
Patty **BERG**	0	1	0	0	0	0	7	7	15
Mickey **WRIGHT**	4	4	0	0	0	0	2	3	13
Louise **SUGGS**	1	2	0	0	0	0	4	4	11
Annika **SÖRENSTAM**	3	3	1	3	0	0	0	0	10
Babe **ZAHARIAS**	0	3	0	0	0	0	3	4	10
Betsy **RAWLS**	2	4	0	0	0	0	0	2	8
Juli **INKSTER**	2	2	0	2	0	1	0	0	7
Inbee **PARK**	3	2	1	1	0	0	0	0	7
Karrie **WEBB**	1	2	1	2	0	1	0	0	7

KEY: LPGA = LPGA Championship, USO = US Open, BO = British Open, ANA = ANA Inspiration, EV = Evian Championship, MAUR = du Maurier (1979–2000), TH = Titleholders (1937–1972), WES = Western Open (1937–1967)

PGA TOUR CAREER EARNINGS*

1.	Tiger Woods	$110,061,012
2.	Phil Mickelson	$83,118,219
3.	Vijay Singh	$70,855,594
4.	Jim Furyk	$67,740,599
5.	Ernie Els	$48,913,269
6.	Sergio Garcia	$46,706,887
7.	Adam Scott	$46,703,451
8.	Dustin Johnson	$45,593,312
9.	Davis Love III	$44,382,824
10.	Steve Stricker	$43,342,350

LPGA TOUR CAREER EARNINGS*

1.	Annika Sorenstam	$22,573,192
2.	Karrie Webb	$20,174,580
3.	Cristie Kerr	$18,538,802
4.	Lorena Ochoa	$14,863,331
5.	Suzann Pettersen	$14,713,350

*Through July 2017

DUSTIN JOHNSON

Dustin Johnson, one of the longest hitters on the PGA Tour, also displayed a nice short touch and a brilliant putting stroke while cracking the career top 10 money list and ascending to No. 1 in the world in 2017. Johnson, the 2016 US Open winner, was unstoppable early in 2017. In February, he won the Genesis Open in Los Angeles. His next time out, he won the World Golf Championships event in Mexico. And his next time out, he won the WGC Match Play event. About the only thing that could slow Johnson down was a back injury that hampered him through the summer.

TENNIS

EIGHT IS GREAT!
At 35 years old, Roger Federer of Switzerland won the singles title at Wimbledon in 2017. He became the first man to win at Wimbledon eight times.

Men's Tennis

Old guys rule! Well, they did in men's tennis in 2017, anyway. And by "old," we mean a group of players in their 30s. In a sport often dominated by players in their teens and early 20s, that seems ancient! Leading the charge was Swiss star **Roger Federer**, whose victory at age 35 in the Australian Open made him the oldest player in 45 years to win a Grand Slam singles title. Several months later, he did it again when he won at Wimbledon.

Federer's huge season came despite entering the year outside the top 10 in the world rankings for the first time in 14 years. (He was No. 16.) The new No. 1 was Great Britain's **Andy Murray**. Early in November 2016, he edged past **Novak Djokovic** in the rankings. Serbia's Djokovic had held the No. 1 spot for an amazing 122 consecutive weeks.

Murray may have been the new No. 1, but there was no single dominant player heading into 2017. Murray, Djokovic, **Stan Wawrinka**, and all-time greats such as Federer and **Rafael Nadal**—all players 30 or older in 2017—could step up in any given tournament.

> **"Being the first male player to reach eight championships here really feels super-special. And I loved having my children here to watch!"**
> — ROGER FEDERER,
> ON WINNING AT WIMBLEDON . . . AGAIN!

With so many contenders, the wide-open draws made for some exciting tennis for fans and television viewers. It started with the first Grand Slam event of the season, the Australian Open. First Djokovic, and then Murray, went down to shocking defeats to unseeded players. That opened the door for Federer and Nadal to make runs to the final. In the championship match, Federer outlasted his long-time rival in an exciting five sets to win his record 18th career major championship.

Then it was the 31-year-old Nadal's turn at the French Open. Nadal was born and raised in Spain, but he's found a second home in Paris. He won the French Open on the famed clay courts of Roland Garros for the record 10th time in 2017. He beat Wawrinka easily in the finals.

Federer, recognizing that clay is not his strongest surface (and that he is not as young as he used to be!) skipped the French Open to stay fresh for Wimbledon. It proved to be a wise decision as he cruised to the final. There he met **Marin Čilić** of Croatia. The final wasn't even close. Federer breezed in three straight sets to win Wimbledon for the record eighth time.

2017 MEN'S GRAND SLAMS

AUSTRALIAN OPEN	**Roger Federer**
FRENCH OPEN	**Rafael Nadal**
WIMBLEDON	**Roger Federer**
US OPEN	**Rafael Nadal**

Women's Tennis

Greatest player ever? The stats say Serena!

Germany's **Angelique Kerber** entered 2017 as the top-ranked women's tennis player in the world. She got there by winning the US Open in the fall of 2016, knocking American **Serena Williams** from the perch she occupied for a record-tying 186 consecutive weeks.

Still, all eyes were on Williams and her bid for a 23rd career Grand Slam title at the 2017 Australian Open. Williams entered the year tied with **Steffi Graf** of Germany for the most titles in the Open Era, which refers to the period beginning in 1968, when professionals first were allowed to compete. (**Margaret Smith Court** holds the all-time record of 24 Grand Slam wins, but 13 of those came before 1968.) Williams quickly ended the suspense, rolling through the bracket in Melbourne. She didn't lose a set in the tournament, including a win over her sister **Venus Williams** in the final. Venus Williams had an impressive year, too. She has been battling a serious illness for years and had not made a Grand Slam final since 2007. Still, she was happy for her younger sister!

After her Australian Open win, Serena hung up her racket and tennis shoes for the year. She announced several months later that she was expecting a baby in September.

Serena's absence opened the door for other stars to step up. At the French Open in Paris, all eight of the quarterfinalists were players looking for their first Grand Slam title. **Jelena Ostapenko** of Latvia beat **Simona Halep** of Romania in three sets in the final.

Then, at Wimbledon, **Garbiñe Muguruza** of Venezuela beat Venus Williams in straight sets to win her second Grand Slam title. After a tense opening set that Muguruza won 7–5, the 23-year-old wore down the 37-year-old Williams, needing only 26 minutes to coast to a 6–0 victory in the clinching set.

2017 WOMEN'S GRAND SLAMS

AUSTRALIAN OPEN	**Serena Williams**
FRENCH OPEN	**Jelena Ostapenko**
WIMBLEDON	**Garbiñe Muguruza**
US OPEN	**Sloane Stephens**

Tennis Notes

NICE RETURNS

While Serena Williams was taking time off for maternity leave, **Victoria Azarenka** of Belarus returned to the court in 2017 after having a baby. Azarenka, who has been ranked as high as No. 7 in the world, missed much of the 2016 season as she prepared for her baby boy's arrival in December. She returned to the courts in June of 2017 and won her opening-round match at the Mallorca Open. The next month, she advanced to the fourth round at Wimbledon.

Former world No. 2 **Petra Kvitova** also made a comeback in 2017. Kvitova is a two-time singles champ at Wimbledon and winner of the bronze medal at the 2016 Olympics in Rio. But she suffered serious hand injuries during a robbery at her home in the Czech Republic in December of 2016. Luckily, she healed in time to play in the French Open in May of 2017, and she beat American **Julia Boserup** in the first round.

INSPIRING WIN ▶▶▶

Alex Hunt, a 23-year-old from New Zealand, won an opening-round match in Guam in the summer of 2017 to earn his first points in the Association of Tennis Professionals (ATP) circuit. What's the big deal about that? Well, Hunt was born with no lower left arm. He plays each match with a prosthetic arm, which he can use only to toss the ball on his serve. Hunt, who was born in a small town on the South Island in New Zealand, never let his physical challenge interfere with his chores on the family farm or with his play on the tennis court. Before turning pro, he played college tennis in the US at St. Mary's in Moraga, California.

READY TO BREAK THROUGH

No American men's tennis player has ranked among the top 10 in the world since **John Isner** in May of 2014. But **Jack Sock**, a native of Lincoln, Nebraska, hopes to end that drought. In the opening three months of 2017, Sock won more matches than any other men's player not named **Roger Federer** or **Rafael Nadal**. He won tournaments in Delray Beach, Florida, and Auckland, New Zealand. And he rose to as high as No. 14 in the world. He was ranked 17th shortly after Wimbledon.

Grand Slams

ALL-TIME GRAND SLAM CHAMPIONSHIPS (MEN)

	AUSTRALIAN	FRENCH	WIMBLEDON	US OPEN	TOTAL
Roger **FEDERER**	5	1	8	5	19
Rafael **NADAL**	1	10	2	3	16
Pete **SAMPRAS**	2	0	7	5	14
Novak **DJOKOVIC**	6	1	3	2	12
Roy **EMERSON**	6	2	2	2	12
Björn **BORG**	0	6	5	0	11
Rod **LAVER**	3	2	4	2	11
Bill **TILDEN**	0	0	3	7	10
Andre **AGASSI**	4	1	1	2	8
Jimmy **CONNORS**	1	0	2	5	8
Ivan **LENDL**	2	3	0	3	8
Fred **PERRY**	1	1	3	3	8
Ken **ROSEWALL**	4	2	0	2	8

ANDRE AGASSI

A native of Las Vegas, Nevada, Andre was one of the top stars of the 1990s. He reached No. 1 in the world in 1995, the same year he won the first of his four Australian Open titles. A devastating forehand stroke—it earned him the nickname "The Punisher"—helped make him one of only eight men to complete a career Grand Slam (winning all four major championships, not necessarily in the same year). Andre is married to former women's tennis great **Steffi Graf**.

ALL-TIME GRAND SLAM CHAMPIONSHIPS (WOMEN)

	AUSTRALIAN	FRENCH	WIMBLEDON	US OPEN	TOTAL
Margaret Smith **COURT**	11	5	3	5	**24**
Serena **WILLIAMS**	7	3	7	6	**23**
Steffi **GRAF**	4	6	7	5	**22**
Helen Wills **MOODY**	0	4	8	7	**19**
Chris **EVERT**	2	7	3	6	**18**
Martina **NAVRATILOVA**	3	2	9	4	**18**
Billie Jean **KING**	1	1	6	4	**12**
Maureen **CONNOLLY**	1	2	3	3	**9**
Monica **SELES**	4	3	0	2	**9**
Suzanne **LENGLEN**	0	2*	6	0	**8**
Molla Bjurstedt **MALLORY**	0	0	0	8	**8**

*Also won four French titles before 1925; in those years, the tournament was open only to French nationals.

Martina Navratilova

No other women's tennis player was as dominant for as long as Navratilova. The Czech-born star (she is now an American citizen) first cracked the top 10 in the world in 1975. Then she stayed there a record 20 years, including 19 of those years in the top 5, and seven— another record—as No. 1. Her 167 career Women's Tennis Association championships are the most in the Open Era. She not only won a record nine Wimbledon singles titles and 18 major singles championships in all, but also is one of the top doubles players ever. Her last championship, in mixed doubles, came at age 49 at the 2006 US Open.

SUDDEN STARS

Prescott set an NFL record by throwing his first 176 passes without an interception!

DAK PRESCOTT
DALLAS COWBOYS

Prescott expected to spend the 2016 NFL season holding a clipboard. After all, backup quarterbacks usually watch from the sidelines. Then Cowboys' starter **Tony Romo** injured his back. Prescott put down his clipboard and pulled on his helmet. It was go time from the first time he stepped on the field on opening weekend. The fourth-round draft pick put a charge into the Cowboys. He led them to 13 wins and was named the NFL Offensive Rookie of the Year!

The sports world welcomes new faces and new heroes every year. They are the young superstars you will be watching for years to come. Look for these athletes on video highlights and learn all about them here, in this new *Year in Sports* feature!

Judge broke the Yankees' rookie record for homers set by the great Joe DiMaggio in 1936!

Bellinger took part in the Home Run Derby. His pitcher was his dad, former MLB player Clay Bellinger.

AARON JUDGE
NEW YORK YANKEES

CODY BELLINGER
LOS ANGELES DODGERS

Baseball fans watched a pair of rookies bust out in 2017—one on each coast. In New York, Judge thrilled fans with tape-measure homers. The fans in the outfield bleachers got to their feet whenever he came up. "All rise!" they shouted, just like when a real judge enters a courtroom! Judge not only smashed homers, but was among the Triple Crown leaders all season. On the West Coast, Bellinger was a bit of a surprise. He took over for an injured starter and started mashing. He reached 21 homers faster than any other player in MLB history! His uppercut swing is a thing of beauty, as long as you're not a baseball!

Embiid hopes to make the 2020 Olympics for Cameroon, either in regular basketball or the new 3-on-3 competition.

JOEL EMBIID
PHILADELPHIA 76ERS

A native of Cameroon, Embiid (pronounced "em-BEED" and pictured here slamming home two points) had to wait a little extra time for his rookie season. The third overall pick in the 2014 draft battled a bad foot injury and had to miss two seasons! Finally, in 2016–17, he took the floor—and took over. Embiid had 19 games with 20 or more points, including a team rookie-record 10 in a row in December and January. He was named to the NBA All-Rookie First Team and looks to help the 76ers reach the playoffs in 2018.

At 18, Pugh was the youngest female player ever in a US Olympic qualifying match.

MALLORY PUGH
US WOMEN'S SOCCER TEAM

American soccer fans have been watching this up-and-coming star, but in 2016 and 2017, the whole world got to see her. A quick and creative striker, Pugh played for the national team when she was only 17, and she scored in her first game! In the summer of 2016, she played for the US in the Olympics. In May 2017, at the age of 19, she was the first overall draft pick in the National Women's Soccer League, by the Washington Spirit. With a Women's World Cup coming in 2019, Pugh is really one to watch.

Connor wears No. 97 because that's the year he was born: 1997!

CONNOR McDAVID
EDMONTON OILERS

Imagine being the captain of the Oilers, the leading goal scorer in the NHL, and the Most Valuable Player. Then imagine signing one of the richest contracts in hockey history—all of this at only 20 years old. Not a bad start. Hockey fans have been enjoying McDavid for years in junior hockey. He was solid as a 19-year-old NHL rookie, but burst out in 2016–17. He was the youngest Oilers captain ever and became only the third player younger than 21 to win the Hart Trophy as MVP. The first two? They were a couple of superstars named **Sidney Crosby** and **Wayne Gretzky**.

Plum not only became the NCAA career scoring leader, she also set a single-season record in 2016–17 with 1,109 points.

KELSEY PLUM
SAN ANTONIO STARS

Plum became women's college basketball's all-time leading scorer during her final game at Washington. Then she was the first overall selection in the WNBA's 2017 draft. She struggled a bit in her early games, but this is a player that never quits. The entire hoops world cheered her on when she set the college points record, and she has the all-around skills to become an all-star at the pro level, too.

SKIING STAR

Having a physical disability hasn't stopped some amazing athletes from capturing world championships. In the Para Alpine events, athletes are matched based on their level of disability. In 2017, Anna Schaffelhuber had a fantastic Para Alpine World Cup season. She racked up enough points in the sitting category to win the overall championship. It was not a big surprise: At the 2014 Winter Paralympics, Schaffelhuber had swept all five gold medals in her sport! For more on other winter sports champions, turn the page!

Winter Sports

World Cup Skiing

World Cup skiing has a new superstar. American slalom expert **Mikaela Shiffrin** won her first overall World Cup title in 2017. In World Cup skiing, racers travel the world throughout the winter. Each weekend, they earn points toward the season-long title. Shiffrin racked up her winning totals by taking first place in slalom and second in giant slalom. She's been a rising star in her specialties, but this was the first time she took the overall title. American **Lindsey Vonn**, already a four-time World Cup champion, became the oldest woman skier to win a medal when she captured the downhill at the world championships in Switzerland. She was only 32, but that's pretty old for world-class skiers!

In the men's World Cup season, the marvelous **Marcel Hirscher** continued his run of success. The Austrian skier has won an amazing six consecutive overall World Cup titles. Like Shiffrin, he's a slalom star. He won that event and giant slalom to pile up an unmatched points total. He finished in the top three in every one of the 12 slalom races, winning four of them.

The World Cup for paralympic athletes—those with physical disabilities—also ranks skiers on points earned over a season. In the Para Alpine Skiing World Cup, there are several categories, based on type of disability. The 2017 men's sitting champion was **Taiki Morii** of Japan. The women's sitting champ was Germany's **Anna Schaffelhuber**.

Shiffrin won her first overall World Cup title by dominating the slalom competition.

Figure Skating

The 2018 Winter Olympics are set for February in South Korea. The 2017 World Figure Skating Championships were a preview of some of the battles on ice that fans will see at the Games.

Russia's **Evgenia Medvedeva** is certainly a gold-medal favorite. In 2017, she won her second world championship in a row, and she's only a teenager! She was the first repeat world champ since 2001.

In the men's singles event, the world title has been passed back and forth. **Yuzuru Hanyu** of Japan and **Javier Fernández** of Spain have each won two of the past four championships. In 2017, Hanyu won his second title with a world-record score. That gives him a boost as he tries to defend his 2014 Olympic gold medal.

In pairs, China's **Sui Wenjing** and **Han Cong** won the gold at the worlds, but they are struggling with injuries, so the Olympic competition could be wide open.

Canada's **Tessa Virtue** and **Scott Moir** won the ice dancing event for the first time since 2012. In the free skate final, they put up the highest score ever awarded. It capped a long comeback that included almost two years away from the ice.

Medvedeva will be only 19 when she goes for gold in 2018.

Speed Skating

Like skiing, the fast-paced sport of speed skating also has a World Cup. Athletes pile up points over a season full of events. They race at distances from 500 to 10,000 meters. In 2017, **Kjeld Nuis** of the Netherlands (right) was the overall World Cup champion. He was also the champ in the 1500 meters, his best race. **Heather Bergsma** of the United States came from behind to win the 1500 and the World Cup title for the women.

America's Cup

There was no comeback this time! In 2013, the US-owned *Oracle* boat made one of the biggest comebacks in sports history. Down 8–1, it won the next eight races to stun the boat from New Zealand and capture the historic America's Cup sailing championship.

In 2017, the Kiwis (that's a nickname for people from New Zealand) didn't let history repeat itself. They won easily, 7–1, in the series of races in the warm waters off Bermuda. At the helm of the 50-foot boat was **Peter Burling**. At 26, he was the youngest "skipper" in the history of the race, which was first held way back in 1851!

New Zealand now controls the Cup and will choose where and when the next races will be held, probably in three years.

AMERICA'S CUP

Here are the last 10 winners:

2017	**New Zealand**
2013	**United States**
2007	**Switzerland**
2003	**Switzerland**
2000	**New Zealand**
1995	**New Zealand**
1992	**United States**
1988	**United States**
1987	**United States**
1983	**Australia**

America's Oracle boat couldn't duplicate its 2013 success and lost to New Zealand.

Lacrosse

INDOOR LACROSSE

The website for the National Lacrosse League called the second game of its championship series "lacrosse heaven." It was certainly dramatic! The NLL plays indoor lacrosse, with six players on a field about the size of a hockey rink. It's a fast-paced, hard-hitting sport with lots of action!

The Georgia Swarm came into the series having set an NLL regular-season record with 116 points. They were led by brothers **Lyle** and **Miles Thompson**. The Swarm's opponent for the championship was the Saskatchewan Rush, and they had a Thompson, too—Lyle and Miles's older brother **Jeremy**.

The finals were best-of-three, and Georgia won the first game. In the second game, the teams battled back and forth in the fourth period. Both were ahead at one point, sometimes scoring just seconds apart. One of the Rush's goals came from Jeremy Thompson. The Rush led with less than 10 seconds remaining, but the Swarm stunned the crowd with a tying goal!

In overtime, Georgia lived up to its name. It swarmed over the Rush. Lyle passed to Miles, who slammed home the championship-winning goal less than a minute into the extra period. That gave them a heavenly 15–14 win!

Swarm captain Jordan MacIntosh

MAJOR LEAGUE LACROSSE

The 2017 Major League Lacrosse championship game was a rematch of the 2016 contest, with one big difference. This year, the 2016 losers came out on top. The Ohio Machine won their first MLL title, 17–12 over the Denver Outlaws. The Machine trailed at halftime, but really turned on the jets in the second half. They came back to tie the game at 12–12 but then scored the final five goals of the game. The first of those five came from MVP **Marcus Holman**, who had four goals and two assists in the game.

Racing, Racing, Racing

Cloud Computing (left) won the Preakness by a head.

The Triple Crown

The winner of the Kentucky Derby had the perfect name for fans of horse racing's Triple Crown. **Always Dreaming** was the favorite in the race, having won two other races leading up to the "Run for the Roses." The track was very muddy after recent rains, so being out front was the safest move. That's where jockey **John Velazquez** steered his horse. Always Dreaming squished through the slop to win by more than two lengths.

So the winning horse's owners were dreaming of a Triple Crown as they watched the Preakness Stakes, the second leg of the Triple Crown. But this dream didn't come true.

For a long time, the Preakness, held near Baltimore, looked like a battle between Always Dreaming and the highly ranked **Classic Empire**. Those two horses were neck and neck down the final straightaway. Their jockeys were so focused on each other they forgot the rest of the field. And from that field raced **Cloud Computing**. Its jockey, **Javier Castellano**, blew loud, smacking kisses toward his horse's ear, and Cloud Computing responded. It burst past the two leading horses. Classic Empire tried to keep up, but Cloud Computing strode to an upset win to end the Triple Crown chances for 2017.

The races went on, however, and horse racing fans looked to the Belmont Stakes. Always Dreaming didn't even enter the race, but its trainer, **Todd Pletcher**, had another horse in his stable. **Tapwrit** stormed past favored **Irish War Cry** to win the longest of the three Triple Crown races. Pletcher was the first trainer since 1996 to win two legs with different horses.

Red Bull Air Racing

It's a bird's-eye view of the Red Bull Air Race!

Flying super-zippy small airplanes, daring pilots take part in the Red Bull Air Racing series. They zing in between gigantic cones and follow a twisting path through the air. They also fly very low to the ground—how else would fans be able to see them? Germany's **Matthias Dolderer** emerged in late 2016 as the season champion. He finished in the top three in each of the seven races. It was no surprise. His parents ran a small airfield in Germany, and he has been flying since he was 14!

F1 Powerboats

A nice cruise on a motorboat is a great way to spend an afternoon. The drivers of F1H2O boats, however, are in it for more than fun. They power high-speed water rockets around twisting courses in search of the championship. In December 2016, French driver **Phillppe Chiappe** won his third F1H2O world title in a row. He finished second to American **Shaun Torrente** in the final race in the United Arab Emirates. Chiappe, however, had enough points to win the season title.

Swimming

Everybody into the pool! Here are some of the highlights of the 2017 World Championships, held in late July in Budapest.

Caeleb's Gold

50-meter freestyle

100-meter freestyle

100-meter butterfly

4x100 freestyle relay

4x100 mixed freestyle relay

4x100-meter medley relay

4x100 mixed medley relay

▲Seven Golds!

American swimmer **Caeleb Dressel** earned seven gold medals at the world championships in Budapest. That matched the record set by the great **Michael Phelps** in 2007. He became the first ever to win three golds in one night! In the space of about two hours, he won the 50-meter freestyle, the 100-meter butterfly, and helped win the mixed 4x100-meter freestyle race. That last was a newer race, in which two men and two women from each country swam 100-meter laps. The US team set a new world record in that event.

Triple Threat

Lilly King was part of three world records during the championships. She set two by herself, in the 50- and 100-meter breaststroke events. Then she joined three teammates in the 4x100-meter medley relay to set a third!

Hometown Hero

Hungary's amazing **Katinka Hosszu** thrilled fans in Budapest. She won her third consecutive 200- and 400-meter individual medley golds. She also won two gold at the 2016 Olympics in Brazil.

Swedish Star

Sarah Sjöström of Sweden carried home an impressive set of medals. She won gold in the 50-meter freestyle race and the 50- and 100-meter butterfly events. She also set a world record in the 100-meter freestyle, which came in the first lap of the 4x100-meter relay. Sweden finished fifth in that event even after Sarah's super start.

Gymnastics

In a year with a Summer Olympics, gymnastics doesn't make the news. It should! The talents on display at the 2017 US Gymnastics Championships in Anaheim, Calif., showed that the next Olympics might be golden for the United States again!

The famous "Final Five" women who won the team event in Rio i 2016–led by all-around champ **Simone Biles**–did not take part in this event. It was time for a new group of stars to emerge.

At that 2016 Olympics, **Ragan Smith** was an alternate, so she just missed out on golden glory. In Anaheim, she stole the show, putting up crisp routines over and over. She came into the event as the big favorite and stood up to the pressure.

"It feels amazing, all of my hard work has paid off," she said. "I'm just excited to be US champion."

Ragan's coach knew how her student felt. **Kim Zmeskal Burdette** captured the 1991 US title on her way to winning the

Ragan Smith shows a championship move.

world championship. After the event was over, Ragan said her next move would be to head down the street to Disneyland "to see the fireworks and stuff!"

On the men's side, it was a Sooner Sweep. Two gymnasts from the University of Oklahoma led the way. **Yul Moldauer** almost saw his title hopes fall when he knocked against one of the parallel bars. But his scores held up for first place. He was just a few points ahead of fellow Sooner **Allan Bower**.

Both US champions hoped for a spot on the World Championship team that competed in October in Montreal.

Other Champs

Gymnastics is more than just the well-known artistic variety. Here are some other US champs in different forms of gymnastics:

EVENT	CHAMP
RHYTHMIC	**Laura ZENG**
TRAMPOLINE	**Nicole AHSINGER** **Jeffrey GLUCKSTEIN**
TUMBLING	**Rachel THEVENOT** **Austin NACEY**

Track & Field

The 2017 Track & Field World Championships were supposed to be the going-away party for one of the sports' greatest all-time heroes. Instead, it turned into a flood of gold for the red, white, and blue.

Gatlin (left) nipped Bolt (in green shorts).

Bolt Fizzles

Usain Bolt of Jamaica is the greatest sprinter of all time. He became the first athlete ever to win Olympic gold in the 100- and 200-meter races three times. In 2017, he announced that the World Championships in London would be his last track meet. Everyone expected him to go out in a blaze of glory. But that didn't happen. In the 100 meters, Bolt lost to American **Justin Gatlin**. Then in the 4x100-meter relay, as Bolt sprinted for the finish line, he suddenly grabbed his leg. He stumbled and then fell, injured and defeated. It was not the ending he wanted. Still, he will be remembered for what he did before he got to London.

Upset City

London got that as its new nickname during these games. Several events featured surprise winners.

* **Ramil Guliyev** of Turkey stunned fans when he beat South Africa's **Wade Van Niekerk** in the 200 meters. Guliyev had never won a medal at a major meet before. Van Niekerk was the defending champion!

* Norway's **Karsten Warholm** was so surprised to win the men's 400-meter hurdles, his first major championship, that he had to check the scoreboard before he started celebrating.

* The US men's 4x400-meter relay team is normally among the most dominant in the world. The US has won nine World golds in this event, including the last six in a row. But in London, Trinidad & Tobago's four-man team surprised everyone by holding off the Americans for the gold.

Bolt by the Numbers

OLYMPIC GOLD MEDALS: **8**

WORLD CHAMPIONSHIP MEDALS: **11**

WORLD RECORD: **9.58**, 100 METERS (SET IN 2009)

WORLD RECORD: **19.19**, 200 METERS (SET IN 2009)

WORLD RECORD: **36.84**, 4X100-METER RELAY (SET IN 2012)

Coburn was a surprise gold medalist.

* France's **Pierre-Ambroise Bosse** surged to the lead in the men's 800-meter race and was surprised that no one caught him. ""It felt like a dream," Bosse said. "You know [in] a nightmare, somebody [is] gonna catch you, but they never catch you, you know?" This dream ended in gold.

* **Mo Farah** had not lost a 5000-meter race in almost eight years . . . until London. **Edris Muktar** of Ethiopia sprinted past Farah on the final lap to win an unexpected gold.

Track Queen

American sprinter **Allyson Felix** is not as famous as Usain Bolt, but she's got more medals than he does! Felix won gold in the 4x100 and 4x400 relays and a bronze in the 400 meters. That gave her 16 career medals in the World Championships, more than any other athlete in the event's history.

American Heroes

US athletes won 30 medals at the World Championships, more than the country ever had won in the event before. The 2017 total included 10 gold, 11 silver, and 9 bronze medals. Here are some of the highlights:

* **Tori Bowie** joined Justin Gatlin in winning 100-meter gold. Bowie was a surprise winner by just 1/100th of a second over **Marie-Josee Ta Lou** of the Ivory Coast.

* **Phyllis Francis** was not expected to challenge for the lead in the 400 meters, but she did more than that—she won. It was her first major international victory.

* **Brittney Reese** leaped just a half-inch beyond 23 feet to win the women's long jump.

◀◀◀ **Sam Kendricks** won the pole vault with a mark of 19 feet, 6.25 inches.

* **Emma Coburn** set an American record, and upset the favored runners from Kenya, while winning the 3000-meter steeplechase.

Amazing Sports

Remarkable sports stories away from the headlines

◄◄◄ Incredible Racer

Completing the mighty Ironman Triathlon (2.4-mile swim, 112-mile bike ride, and a marathon . . . one after the other!) is a huge task. But an Australian woman named **Turia Pitt** amazed even the Ironman's super-fit racers. Pitt was horribly injured in a fire in 2011. She lost most of her fingers and spent more than two years in a hospital. But she got out, started training, and, in 2016, she completed the Ironman to the cheers of thousands. Truly amazing!

Sailor Man ▶▶▶

Sailing around the world has been a goal for many ever since folks realized it could be done! Explorers first made the journey hundreds of years ago, and the trip usually took months or even years. Since then, high-speed, high-tech sailing machines have tried to shorten that journey. In 2017, French sailor **Thomas Coville** might have become the fastest yet. Leaving from the English Channel, he returned to Brest, France, in just over 49 days!

Speed Bowling!

A perfect game in bowling is pretty rare. It means throwing strikes in all 10 frames—including three strikes in the last frame for a total of 12—to reach a final score of 300. Before 2017, everyone who had bowled such a game did it on one lane. **Ben Ketola** did something different. He tossed a strike on 10 lanes, one after the other. Then he ran back to the start and threw two more. A perfect game . . . and it only took him 86.9 seconds!

RUNNING MAN

Running one marathon is a challenge. That's 26.2 miles without stopping. The best can do it in a little over two hours. But then they need weeks of rest. **Michael Wardian** outdid all of them. In January of 2017, Wardian ran seven marathons in seven days . . . on seven continents! And he didn't just run—he WON all seven. Wardian was part of a group of more than 30 runners who took part in the World Marathon Challenge. Special flights took the runners from place to place. They landed, ran, and hopped back on the plane! The map shows their amazing route.

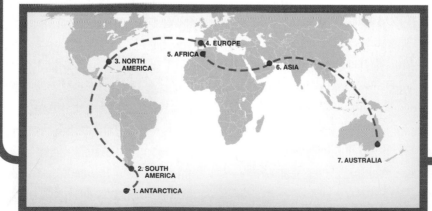

4. EUROPE

5. AFRICA

3. NORTH AMERICA

6. ASIA

7. AUSTRALIA

2. SOUTH AMERICA

1. ANTARCTICA

Games People Play

Not every sport makes the highlight shows. Some are a bit less well-known. Here are some sports that were big news . . . away from the headlines.

▲ Ultimate!

How big has this sport become? Ultimate now has a pro league, a national club championship, and events in several college divisions. Amazing plays appear regularly on ESPN's Top Plays, and kids are now playing in PE classes nationwide. In Ultimate, players throw and catch a flying disc sort of like a football. But the action never stops, like in soccer. It's fun and action-packed and very cool. There are not even any referees (except in top pro events); players call their own fouls!

Chess Gold

Okay, it's not really a sport, but the United States did win an important chess title. In late 2016, four players combined to win gold at the Chess Olympiad. The team was led by **Wesley So**, ranked seventh in the world. He was joined by **Fabiano Caruana**, **Hikaru Nakamura**, **Sam Shankland**, and **Ray Robson**. So did not lose once in the two-week-long event and won the individual gold medal as well. Teams from more than 180 countries took place, and it was the Americans' first gold medal in 40 years!

▲ Spikeball

One magazine writer said that if you combine volleyball with four-square you'd get this game: spikeball. It's been around for more than 30 years, but only in the last few has this fun game really gotten hot. You play with four people around a small, bouncy net. Each team gets three hits per turn, like volleyball. You try to hit the ball so your opponents can't return it. It's gotten so popular that there arc national championship events for teams and for colleges!

Darts? Yes . . . Darts!

The game looks so easy on your rec room wall, but then you try it . . . and you realize that darts is harder than it looks! The game is hugely popular in England and some other European countries. Championship matches on TV draw big ratings. In the United States, it's not quite that big a deal. However, millions of people play. National events such as the USA Classic draw the best throwers. In 2017, **Larry Butler** and **Paula Murphy** won the men's and women's titles. **Tyler Burnett** and **Jenna Yazbek** were the junior champs.

Drone Racing League

Those whirling drones are good for more than just taking amazing aerial photos. They race, too! Expert pilots send high-speed drone flyers around maze-like courses. In August 2017, the Drone Racing League held its world championships. Flying his machine at more than 80 miles per hour, **Jordan "Jet" Temkin** held on to win the world title. He also won in 2016!

NCAA Highlights: Men

College sports doesn't end with football and basketball. The NCAA hosts championships in four divisions and dozens of sports for men and women (and even co-ed, such as fencing and rifle shooting). Here are some highlights from college sports that might not have made *SportsCenter*.

greatest college distance runners ever. Although a back injury kept him from participating in the NCAA Outdoor Championships his senior season in 2017, he finished his career as the winningest runner in NCAA history. He won a combined 17 NCAA titles in cross country, indoor track and field, and outdoor track and field.

Hat Trick

Jarid Lukosevicius scored all of his team's goals—and all of them in the second period—as the University of Denver defeated Minnesota Duluth 3–2 in the 2017 NCAA men's ice hockey final in Chicago. The Pioneers, a traditional college powerhouse in winter sports, won their eighth national championship. Their eight hockey titles are tied with North Dakota for the second most among all schools, behind only Michigan's nine.

King Ches ▲

The legend of runner **Edward Cheserek** ("King Ches") began when he was a teenager in his native Kenya. Given a shot at attending prep school in the United States, the 16-year-old had to pass an entrance test. The exam was no problem, but getting there was. He had to travel 60 miles to the test site, and the roads were washed out. So what did he do? He ran, of course! The rest is history.

Cheserek eventually earned a scholarship to the University of Oregon, where he became one of the

Red Berenson, the head coach who led Michigan to two of those championships, retired at the end of the 2017 season. Berenson is a native of Saskatchewan, Canada, and a former NHL star. He guided the Wolverines for 33 seasons. He finished with a career coaching record of 848–429–92.

Finally a Champ ▲▲

Florida won its first NCAA baseball crown by sweeping two games from LSU in a best-of-three final in the 2017 College World Series. The Tigers made it to the final by handing top-ranked Oregon State its first back-to-back losses in more than a year. But the Gators' pitching and defense was too much for them. It was Florida's first-ever baseball championship after reaching 10 previous World Series.

Relay Rally ▶▶

AJ Digby helped Mount Union to a dramatic victory in the 4 x 400 men's relay at the NCAA Division III Track and Field Championships in Geneva, Ohio, in May 2017. Digby passed three opposing runners over the final lap to give the Raiders the win. Even more dramatic? Digby runs with artificial legs. He was born with a rare disease and first was fitted for prosthetic legs when he was one year old. Digby, a freshman in 2017 who also reached the finals of the individual 400 meter finals at the NCAA indoor meet, competed for the US at the 2016 Paralympic Games in Rio, Brazil.

NCAA Highlights: Women

Strike Zone

It's not often that the "Davids" of the college sports world—the smaller NCAA Division II and Division III schools—get a chance to square off against the "Goliaths"—the larger Division I schools. Competition and championships are separate in most sports. But in bowling, the NCAA holds one championship for all divisions.

In 2017, little-known McKendree University of Lebanon, Illinois, became the first Division II school to win the NCAA bowling title. The private liberal arts school of 2,300 undergraduates swept five-time national champ Nebraska, a state public school with more than 50,000 students. Freshman **Breanna Clemmer** threw the decisive strikes in the final frame for McKendree.

Pitch Perfect ▶▶▶

After pitcher **Paige Parker** led Oklahoma to college softball's national championship, she threw out the first pitch at a Kansas City Royals game. Parker, who is from Independence, Missouri, went 26–5 as the Sooners won their second consecutive Women's College World Series in 2017. Parker was named to the WCWS All-Tournament team for the second year in a row. (She was the WCWS MVP in 2016.)

Not long after, Paige was invited to toss the first pitch when the Royals hosted the Boston Red Sox at Kauffman Stadium. Not surprisingly, the pitch was a strike down the middle. But what really opened eyes was video of a warm-up session before the first pitch that circulated widely on social media. Parker almost knocked over Royals catcher **Drew Butera** with her blazing fastball.

Weather or Not

It's usually not a good sign when the weather at an event overshadows the event itself. That's what happened at the NCAA Division I Women's Golf Championship in Sugar Grove, Illinois. The event was less about birdies and bogies than it was about wind and rain.

After a heavy downpour and 20-mile-per-hour winds cut 18 holes from the qualifying rounds (Northwestern won with an unusually high score of 33 over par for only

Arizona State weathered the storm.

performance at the 2016 Olympics in Rio. Then she enrolled at Stanford to begin college in the 2016–17 academic year. Ledecky, who won four golds among her five medals in Brazil, picked up right where she left off. She won five NCAA titles and led Stanford's women's team to its first national championship since 1998. At season's end, she was named the Collegiate Woman Athlete of the Year.

three rounds), the top teams advanced to match play. Arizona State outlasted seven other schools—and the elements—to win its record eighth national title. The Sun Devils beat Northwestern 3.5–1.5 in the final.

Swim Star

Remember **Katie Ledecky**? The then-19-year-old US swimmer became a beloved star across America with her

2 The number of national championships won by USC in beach volleyball. Of course, there have only been two, so USC has won *all* of them! The duo of junior **Terese Cannon** and senior **Nicolette Martin** edged Pepperdine 15–13 in the final set to give the Trojans a 3–2 win.

Ledecky did for the Stanford swim team what she did for the US Olympic team: win!

Big Events 2017-18

September 2017

7 Basketball
WNBA Playoffs begin

7 Football
NFL regular season begins
with a matchup between the
Kansas City Chiefs and the
New England Patriots

9–10 Tennis
US Open finals,
New York, New York

16–24 Cycling
Road World Cycling
Championships, Bergen,
Norway

24– **Rowing**
Oct. 1 World Championships,
Sarasota, Florida

28– **Golf**
Oct. 1 Presidents Cup,
Jersey City, New Jersey

October 2017

2–8 Gymnastics
World Artistic Gymnastics
Championships, Montreal,
Canada

3 Baseball
MLB postseason begins
(Wild Card playoff games,
League Division Series,
League Championship Series,
World Series)

4 Ice Hockey
NHL regular season begins

14 Swim/Bike/Run
Ironman Triathlon World
Championship, Kailua-Kona,
Hawaii

17 Basketball
NBA regular season begins

TBA Ice Hockey
NWHL regular season begins

November 2017

5 Running
New York City Marathon

12–19 Tennis
ATP World Tour Finals,
London, England

19 Stock Car Racing
Ford EcoBoost 400, final race
of NASCAR Chase for the
Cup, Homestead, Florida

26 Auto Racing
Abu Dhabi Grand Prix,
final race of Formula 1 season

26 Football
Grey Cup, CFL Championship
Game, Ottawa, Canada

December 2017

1 College Football
Pac-12 Championship Game,
Santa Clara, California

1 Soccer
Final draw for the 2018 World
Cup, Moscow, Russia

1, 3 College Soccer
Women's College Cup,
Orlando, Florida

2 College Football

ACC Championship Game,
Charlotte, NC

Big 12 Championship Game,
Arlington, Texas

Big Ten Championship Game,
Indianapolis, Indiana

SEC Championship Game,
Atlanta, Georgia

7–16 Rodeo
National Finals Rodeo,
Las Vegas, Nevada

8–10 College Soccer
Men's College Cup,
Philadelphia, Pennsylvania

29 College Football
Cotton Bowl, Arlington, Texas

29– Figure Skating
Jan. 8 US Figure Skating
Championships,
San Jose, California

30 College Football
Fiesta Bowl, Glendale,
Arizona

Orange Bowl, Miami, Florida

TBA Soccer
MLS Cup,
Site and date TBA

January 2018

1 College Football

College Football Playoff
Semifinal; Rose Bowl,
Pasadena, California

College Football Playoff
Semifinal; Sugar Bowl,
New Orleans, Louisiana

Peach Bowl, Atlanta, Georgia

6–7 Football
NFL Wild Card Playoff
Weekend

8 College Football
College Football
Championship Game,
Atlanta, Georgia

13–14 Football
NFL Divisional Playoff
Weekend

21 Football
NFL Conference Title Games

25–28 Action Sports
Winter X Games, Aspen,
Colorado

27–28 Tennis
Australian Open finals

28 Hockey
NHL All-Star Game,
Tampa, Florida

28 Football
NFL Pro Bowl,
Orlando, Florida

February 2018

4 Football
Super Bowl LII, Minneapolis,
Minnesota

9–25 Winter Olympic Games
PyeongChang, South Korea

18 Basketball
NBA All-Star Game,
Los Angeles, California

18 Stock Car Racing
(NASCAR) Daytona 500,
Daytona Beach, Florida

TBA Baseball
Caribbean Series, Mexico

March 2018

8–18 Winter Paralympics
PyeongChang, South Korea

19–25 Figure Skating
World Figure Skating
Championships,
Milan, Italy

30– College Basketball
April 1 NCAA Women's Final Four,
Columbus, Ohio

31– College Basketball
April 2 NCAA Men's Final Four,
San Antonio, Texas

April 2018

2 Baseball
Major League Baseball,
Opening Day

5–8 Golf
The Masters,
Augusta, Georgia

TBA Ice Hockey
NHL playoffs begin

May 2018

4–20 Ice Hockey
IIHF World Championships,
Copenhagen and Herning,
Denmark

5 Horse Racing
Kentucky Derby, Churchill
Downs, Louisville, Kentucky

19 Horse Racing
Preakness Stakes,
Pimlico Race Course,
Baltimore, Maryland

26 Soccer
UEFA Champions League Final,
Kiev, Ukraine

27 IndyCar Racing
Indianapolis 500,
Indianapolis, Indiana

27– **Tennis**
June 10 French Open, Paris, France

31– **Golf**
June 3 US Women's Open,
Shoal Creek, Alabama

June 2018

9 Horse Racing
Belmont Stakes, Belmont Park,
Elmont, New York

14–17 Golf
US Open Championship,
Southampton, New York

14– **Soccer**
July 15 World Cup, Russia

16 College Baseball
College World Series begins,
Omaha, Nebraska

28– **Golf**
July 1 Women's PGA Championship,
Kildeer, Illinois

30 Cycling
Tour de France begins,
Noirmoutier-en-l'Île, France

TBA Basketball
NBA Finals begin

July 2018

10 Baseball
MLB All-Star Game,
Washington, DC

14–15 Tennis
Wimbledon Championships
finals, London, England

19–22 Action Sports
Summer X Games,
Minneapolis, Minnesota

19–22 Golf
British Open Championship,
Carnoustie, Scotland

20–22 Rugby
World Cup Sevens,
San Francisco, California

21– **Field Hockey**
Aug. 5 Women's Hockey World Cup,
London, England

August 2018

9–12 Golf
PGA Championship,
St. Louis, Missouri

TBA Baseball
Little League World Series,
Williamsport, Pennsylvania

Note: Dates and sites subject to change. TBA: To be announced. Actual dates of event not available at press time.

Produced by Shoreline Publishing Group LLC

Santa Barbara, California

www.shorelinepublishing.com

President/Editorial Director: James Buckley, Jr.

Designed by Tom Carling, www.carlingdesign.com

The *Scholastic Year in Sports* text was written by **James Buckley, Jr.**

Editorial assistance and text for Golf/Tennis/Action Sports: **Jim Gigliotti.**

Fact-checking: **Matt Marini.** Thanks to **Beth Adelman, Zachary Vanderberg,**

and **Craig Zeichner** for their help with the NHL chapter.

Thanks to Paige Hazzan, Maya Frank-Levine, Jael Fogle, Bonnie Cutler, Deborah Kurosz, Emily Teresa, Samantha Swank, and the superstars at Scholastic for all their championship work! Photo research was done by the author.

Photography Credits

Photos ©: cover top left: Minas Panagiotakis/Getty Images; cover top right: Leon Bennett/Getty Images; cover center left: Nick Wass/AP Images; cover center right: Damian Strohmeyer/AP Images; cover bottom center: Chris Szagola/AP Images; cover bottom center: Laurence Griffiths/Getty Images; cover center bottom right: Jason Heidrich/AP Images; cover bottom right: dpa picture alliance/Alamy Images; back cover right: Visionhaus/Getty Images; back cover bottom: Paul Bereswill/Getty Images; 4: Matthew Emmons/USA Today Sports; 5: Yomiuri Shimbun/AP Images; 7 top left, 8: Gregory Vasil/AP Images; 7 top center, 9: Matthew Emmons/USA Today Sports; 7 top right, 10: Kieran McManus/REX/Shutterstock/AP Images; 7 center left, 11: Presse Sports/USA Today Sports; 7 center, 12: Mark D. Smith/USA Today Sports; 7 center right, 13: Chris Carlson/AP Images; 7 bottom left, 14: John David Mercer/USA Today Sports; 7 bottom center, 15: The Greenville News/USA Today Sports; 7 bottom right, 16–17: Monica M. Davey/AP Images; 18–19: Charles LeClaire/USA Today Sports; 20–21: Richard Mackson/USA Today Sports; 22: Cary Edmondson/USA Today Sports; 24: Peter Read Miller/AP Images; 25: LM Otero/AP Images; 26: Jason Getz/USA Today Sports; 27: Dan Powers/USA Today Sports; 28: Mark J. Rebilas/USA Today Sports; 29: Jayne Kamin-Oncea/USA Today Sports; 30: Eric Hartline/USA Today Sports; 31: Jasen Vinlove/USA Today Sports; 32: Scott R. Galvin/USA Today Sports; 33: Detroit Lions/AP Images; 34: Mark J. Rebilas/USA Today Sports; 35: Kirby Lee/USA Today Sports; 38–39: Streeter Lecka/Getty Images; 40: Lisa Blumenfeld/Getty Images; 41: Rich Graessle/AP Images; 42: Mark Humphrey/AP Images; 43: Icon Sportswire/Getty Images; 44: Greg Bartram/USA Today Sports; 45: Aaron Doster/USA Today Sports; 46: Kirby Lee/USA Today Sports; 47: Paul Spinelli/AP Images; 48: Jason Getz/USA Today Sports; 49: Kevin C. Cox/Getty Images; 52–53: Patrick Gorski/USA Today Sports; 54: Joshua Sarner/AP Images; 55: Peter Joneleit/Cal Sport Media/AP Images; 56: Chris Young/AP Images; 58: Nam Y. Huh/AP Images; 59: Dick Druckman/AP Images; 60: Neville E. Guard/USA Today Sports; 61: Isaiah J. Downing/USA Today Sports; 62: Jordan Johnson/USA Today Sports; 63: Adam Hunger/USA Today Sports; 64: Jesse Johnson/USA Today Sports; 65 top: Brian Rothmuller/AP Images; 65 bottom: Robert Hanashiro/USA Today Sports; 68–69: Matthew Emmons/USA Today Sports; 70: Thomas J. Russo/USA Today Sports; 71: Jay Biggerstaff/USA Today Sports; 72: Thomas J. Russo/USA Today Sports; 73: Mike Granse/USA Today Sports; 74: Brian Spurlock/USA Today Sports; 75: Bob Donnan/USA Today Sports; 76: Aaron Doster/USA Today Sports; 77 top: Eric Gay/AP Images; 77 bottom: Matthew Emmons/USA Today Sports; 80–81: Pool Photo/USA Today Sports; 82: Mark D. Smith/USA Today Sports; 83: Mark D. Smith/USA Today Sports; 84: Brad Mills/USA Today Sports; 85: Bob Donnan/USA Today Sports; 86: Paul Zimmerman/Getty Images; 87: Mark J. Rebilas/USA Today Sports; 88: Kyle Terada/USA Today Sports; 89 top: Bob Donnan/USA Today Sports; 89 bottom: Bob DeChiara/USA Today Sports; 90: Ross D. Franklin/AP Images; 91: Jayne Kamin-Oncea/USA Today Sports; 94–95: Gene J. Puskar/AP Images; 96: John E. Sokolowski/USA Today Sports; 97: Aaron Doster/USA Today Sports; 98: Perry Nelson/USA Today Sports; 99: Jeff Roberson/AP Images; 100: Perry Nelson/USA Today Sports; 101 top: Jerry Lai/USA Today Sports; 101 bottom: Chris Szagola/AP Images; 102: Dan Hamilton/USA Today Sports; 103: Carlos Osorio/AP Images; 104: Stan Szeto/USA Today Sports; 105: Geoff Burke/USA Today Sports; 108–109: Anadolu Agency/Getty Images; 110: Trask Smith/AP Images; 111: Geoff Burke/USA Today Sports; 112 top: Etsuo Hara/Getty Images; 112 bottom: Angel Martinez/Getty Images; 113: NurPhoto/Getty Images; 114: Witters Sport/USA Today Sports; 115: Thaiview/Dreamstime; 118–119: Jasen Vinlove/USA Today Sports; 120: Kevin Hoffman/USA Today Sports; 122: Rainier Ehrhardt/AP Images; 123: Mark J. Rebilas/USA Today Sports; 124: Michael Shroyer/USA Today Sports; 125: Michael Shroyer/USA Today Sports; 126: Icon Sportswire/Getty Images; 127 top: Jasen Vinlove/USA Today Sports; 127 bottom: Chuck Burton/AP Images; 130–131: David Davies/AP Images; 132: Kirill Kudryavtsev/Getty Images; 133: Moises Castillo/AP Images; 134: Eric Risberg/AP Images; 135: Michael Conroy/AP Images; 136: David Allio/AP Images; 137: fotopress/Getty Images; 140–141: Icon Sportswire/Getty Images; 142: David Berding/AP Images; 143: Aaron Lavinsky/TNS/Newscom; 144: RJ Sangosti/Getty Images; 146: Courtesy Red Bull Media Content Pool; 147: Francisco Leong/Getty Images; 148: Peter Morrison/AP Images; 149: Matt Slocum/AP Images; 150: Charles Rex Arbogast/AP Images; 151: David Davies/AP Images; 152: John Bazemore/AP Images; 153 top: Cindy Ellen Russell/AP Images; 153 bottom: Alastair Grant/AP Images; 156: Cynthia Lum/AP Images; 158: GEPA/USA Today Sports; 159: Roberto Schmidt/Getty Images; 160: Christof Stache/AP Images; 161: Dave Caulkin/AP Images; 162: Jerome Miron/USA Today Sports; 163 left: Andy Marlin/USA Today Sports; 163 right: Mark J. Terrill/AP Images; 164: Mark J. Rebilas/USA Today Sports; 165: Matthew Emmons/USA Today Sports; 166: Perry Nelson/USA Today Sports; 167: Eric Gay/AP Images; 168–169: Andrea Spinelli/Getty Images; 170: Jeff Swinger/USA Today Sports; 171 top: Daniel Mihailescu/Getty Images; 171 bottom: Sergei Belski/USA Today Sports; 172: Gregory Bull/AP Images; 173: Courtesy Georgia Swarm; 174: Matt Slocum/AP Images; 175 top: Handout/Getty Images; 175 bottom: Homydesign/Dreamstime; 176: Jens B'ttner/AP Images; 177: Gary A. Vasquez/USA Today Sports; 178: Ug Co. K/REX/Shutterstock/AP Images; 179 top: Giuliano Bevilacqua/Sipa USA/AP Images; 179 center: Kirby Lee/USA Today Sports; 180 top: Sean M. Haffey/Getty Images; 180 bottom: Aurora Photos/Alamy Images; 181 top: Mark Conlon/World Marathon Challenge; 183 top: Sandra Foyt/Dreamstime; 183 bottom: Barcroft Media/Getty Images; 184: Kirby Lee/USA Today Sports; 185 top: Kevin Jairaj/USA Today Sports; 185 bottom: Courtesy University of Mount Union; 186: Sarah Phipps/AP Images; 187 top: Patrick Gorski/AP Images; 187 bottom: Zach Bolinger/AP Images.